Windows 3.1 Quick & Easy Reference

Windows™ 3.1
Quick & Easy Reference

Douglas Hergert

San Francisco
Paris
Düsseldorf
Soest

SYBEX®

Acquisitions Editor: Dianne King
Developmental Editor: Richard Mills
Editor: Guy Hart-Davis
Technical Editor: Erik Ingenito
Chapter Art and Typesetting: Guy Hart-Davis
Proofreader/Production Assistant: Janet K. Boone
Indexer: Liz Cunningham
Cover Designer: Archer Design
Cover Illustrator: Richard Miller

Screen reproductions produced with Collage Plus.

Collage Plus is a trademark of Inner Media Inc.

SYBEX is a registered trademark of SYBEX Inc.

TRADEMARKS: SYBEX has attempted throughout this book to distinguish proprietary trademarks from descriptive terms by following the capitalization style used by the manufacturer.

SYBEX is not affiliated with any manufacturer.

Every effort has been made to supply complete and accurate information. However, SYBEX assumes no responsibility for its use, nor for any infringement of the intellectual property rights of third parties which would result from such use.

Library of Congress Card Number: 9385944

ISBN: 0-7821-1377-X

Manufactured in the United States of America

10 9 8 7 6 5 4 3 2 1

ACKNOWLEDGMENTS

My sincere thanks to Guy Hart-Davis, Richard Mills, Joanne Cuthbertson, and Rudolph Langer for their ideas and suggestions; and to the following people for their contributions: Erik Ingenito, technical editor; Janet Boone, proofreader/production assistant; and Liz Cunningham, indexer. Thanks also to Claudette Moore, of Moore Literary Agency.

TABLE OF CONTENTS

xii

INTRODUCTION

Windows 3.1 turns your screen into a visual "desktop," a consistent and dependable environment for all the work you do on your computer. In major software categories—such as word processing, spreadsheets, database management, graphics, and even entertainment—Windows programs have become standards for personal computing.

Windows 3.1 Quick & Easy Reference is designed to provide fast answers to everyday questions about Windows and its applications. Whatever the task you're faced with—starting a program, creating a document, arranging the desktop, changing a setting, or just finding your way from one window to another—this little book provides concise and simple instructions for getting it done. Along the way, you'll find advice, reminders, shortcuts, tips, technical hints, and occasional warnings.

The book is organized in five parts:

> Part 1 introduces general operations on the Windows desktop and basic tasks you perform with the mouse and the keyboard.

> Part 2 shows you how to use the Program Manager to organize your work in Windows.

> Part 3 provides instructions for using applications that come with Windows, including Calendar, Cardfile, Paintbrush, Write, and several others, arranged in alphabetical order.

Part 4 presents the File Manager, the *system application* designed to help you work with disks and files on your computer.

Part 5 is a guide to the Control Panel, the application in which you can change the way Windows looks and behaves on your computer.

To help you look up information quickly and efficiently, you'll find a list of major topics printed on the inside cover, and a detailed index at the end.

Part 1

Basic Tasks in Windows

Introduction

Windows has its own terms for describing the events and items that you see on the screen. This vocabulary is mostly intuitive, although Windows uses several unlikely metaphors that can confuse or amuse a newcomer to the software. (How can a desktop have windows? How can you scroll a window?) Here is a review of some common Windows terms you'll come across in Part 1 of this book:

- An *application* is a program that you use in Windows. Windows applications include business software—such as word processors, spreadsheets, database management programs—as well as entertainment and educational programs. When you are ready to work in an application, you *start* it (or *run* it) from Windows.

- A *document* is an individual piece of work that you create with a Windows application—for example, a letter in a word-processing program, a table of numbers and formulas in a spreadsheet program, or a collection of company names, addresses, phone numbers, and logos in a database management program. On disk, each document is generally saved in its own file.

- A *window* is a framed rectangular area on the screen, designed for your work in a particular application. Each application you run appears in its own window. Because you can run more than one application at a time, you may have many open windows on your screen. The *active* application—among those that are running—is the window in which you are currently working. Within an application window, an open document appears in its own window. Some Windows applications allow you to open multiple documents at once, but others allow only one open document at a time.

- The *desktop* is the entire work area of the screen. By default the desktop background is gray, but you can change it to a different color or pattern if you want to. You arrange your work on the desktop in any way that suits you, by moving windows to new locations and by changing their sizes.

- An icon is a small picture of an application or a group of applications. Application windows can be *minimized* into icons, and icons can be *restored* to their corresponding application windows. An icon on the desktop represents a running application that you have temporarily placed out of the way of your other work.

- The *mouse pointer* is a small white arrow representing the movements of the mouse attached to your computer. (Sometimes the mouse pointer takes on other shapes that you'll learn to recognize as you work in Windows and applications.) Many tasks in Windows are easiest to perform with the mouse, but often there are shortcuts and alternate techniques that you can accomplish on the keyboard.

- Finally, *Program Manager* is a primary component of Windows that is always present on the desktop, either as an open window or as an icon. Program Manager shows you the applications available and gives you simple ways to choose activities. The Program Manager window contains *group icons* and *group windows* that represent categories of applications. It also contains *menus* of commands that you can choose to carry out particular tasks in Windows. (You'll be able to use the Program Manager window to experiment with several of the tasks described in Part 1. Part 2 of this book focuses specifically on Program Manager.)

Figure 1.1 will help you understand this basic vocabulary, along with some other terms that you'll learn in the entries ahead.

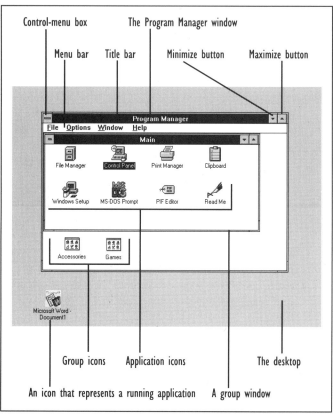

FIGURE 1.1: *The elements of the desktop when you first start Windows*

The entries in Part 1 show you how to perform some important general tasks in Windows, such as arranging items on the
desktop, starting applications, and switching from one application to another. You'll find yourself doing these things almost
every time you work in Windows, no matter what your main
activity is.

Starting Windows

The most straightforward way to start Windows is simply to enter **win** from the DOS prompt. When Windows starts, the Program Manager window appears on the desktop. (If all you see is the Program Manager icon, move the mouse pointer over the icon and double-click the left mouse button. See *Using the Mouse* on page 9 for more information about double-clicking.)

You can also enter additional instructions on the **win** command line. Most commonly, you can identify an application that will be run immediately as soon as Windows gets started.

To Start Windows and Immediately Run an Application

Enter the **win** command line from the DOS prompt as follows:

```
C>win ApplicationName
```

For example, the following command starts Windows and then immediately starts Microsoft Word for Windows:

```
C>win winword
```

 **techno note**

You can also specify the mode in which Windows will be run—the standard mode or the 386 enhanced mode. In general, the standard mode is for 286-based computers, and the 386 enhanced mode is for 386- or 486-based computers. Windows normally determines the appropriate mode for your system, but you may sometimes want to override this decision. For example, to improve performance, you might choose to run Windows in standard mode even if your system meets the requirements for the 386 enhanced mode.

To Start Windows
in Standard or Enhanced Mode

Enter the **win** command in the following form for standard mode:

```
C>win /S
```

or in the following form for 386 enhanced mode:

```
C>win /3
```

 tip

In these two command lines, /S and /3 are known as *switches*. A switch activates an available mode or feature of a program. If you want to see the other switches available for the Windows command line, type the following command from the DOS prompt:

```
C>win /?
```

This command does not start Windows. Instead, it displays an instruction screen showing you the various switches you can use to start Windows.

To Start Windows Automatically When You Turn on Your Computer

Enter **win** as the final line of text in your AUTOEXEC.BAT file. This text file is located in the *root directory* of your hard disk. (See Part 4, *File Manager*, for general information about directories.) AUTOEXEC.BAT lists DOS commands to be performed initially whenever you turn on your computer.)

To edit the AUTOEXEC.BAT file, you can use any text processor—including the EDIT utility that comes with DOS, or the Windows Notepad application. After you add this **win** line to AUTOEXEC.BAT, Windows will start each time you turn on your computer.

Exiting Windows

To quit Windows and return to DOS, you might typically want to begin by closing all the applications currently open on the desktop. To do this, you switch to each application in turn, and close its window. (See *Closing an Application* on page 19 for details.) Finally, to exit Windows itself, you close the Program Manager window.

Alternatively, you can switch directly to Program Manager at any time, and close its window to quit Windows. If other applications are still running, Windows closes them before completing the exit.

 tip

If there are any unsaved documents in a running application— that is, if there are changes that you have not yet saved to disk— Windows asks you if you want to save the changes before exiting.

To Return to Program Manager from an Application

1. Press Ctrl+Esc to open the Task List. (Or position the mouse pointer over any background area of the desktop and double-click the left mouse button.)

2. Select Program Manager in the Task List.

3. Click the Switch To button.

If you have made changes in the arrangement of items in the Program Manager window, you have the choice of saving the new arrangement for your next Windows session or of reverting to the previous arrangement.

To Save the Program Manager Arrangement Before You Exit

1. Click Options in the Program Manager menu bar (or press Alt and then O) to pull down the Options menu.

2. If no check mark (✓) appears to the left of the Save Settings on Exit command, choose this command to toggle the option on. (If a check mark already appears, press Esc twice to close the menu without changing the setting.)

When this setting is on, Windows saves the current Program Manager arrangement for the next session. Now you are ready to quit Windows.

To Close Program Manager and Exit Windows

1. Pull down the File menu from the Program Manager menu bar.

2. Choose the Exit Windows command from the File menu. An Exit Windows dialog box appears on the screen, asking you to confirm your action.

3. Click the OK button or press Enter from the keyboard to confirm. (Click the Cancel button or press Esc if you change your mind about exiting Windows.)

 reminder

You can also use the control-menu box to close the Program Manager window, as described in *Closing an Application* (page 19).

When you quit Windows, the screen clears and you return immediately to the DOS prompt.

Using the Mouse

The three actions you perform most commonly with the mouse are known as *clicking*, *double-clicking*, and *dragging*. The result of any one of these actions depends upon the item you have selected on the desktop.

warning

Unfortunately, the vocabulary used to describe mouse actions can be ambiguous and inconsistent from one Windows application to the next. You'll see books that refer to *selecting*, *choosing*, and *activating* an item with the mouse, but you may not always be certain about the distinction among these actions. In the Windows documentation, *selecting* usually means activating or highlighting an object, and *choosing* usually means carrying out an action related to an object. Depending on the context, these terms may refer to either a single mouse click or a double-click. As you begin using new applications in Windows, make sure you understand the exact mouse actions that are required for particular results.

tip

By default, the left mouse button is the one you use for major activities on the desktop, and the right mouse button is reserved for special actions defined by applications. But Windows allows you to reverse the roles of the left and right mouse buttons, which you might want to do if you are left-handed; see *Mouse Settings* in Part 5 of this book for instructions. This book refers to the default left mouse button as the one to use for performing common mouse actions.)

To Run an Application by Choosing Its Icon

1. In Program Manager, move the mouse pointer over the icon for the application you want to run.

2. Click the left mouse button twice quickly in succession.
This is called *double-clicking*. In response, Windows opens
the application's window onto the desktop.

 tip

You can reset the speed required for a successful double-click.
See *Mouse Settings* in Part 5 for information.

 reminder

If an application is already running but displayed as an icon on
the desktop, you can restore the application window by
double-clicking the icon. See *Running an Application* on page 14
for more information.

To Activate a Window

1. Move the mouse pointer anywhere inside the window.

2. Click the left mouse button once.

 reminder

The active application window is the one that you are
currently working in. Only one window is active at a time.

To Drag an Icon

1. Move the mouse pointer over the icon.

2. Hold down the left mouse button and move the icon to a new position on the desktop.

3. Release the mouse button to complete the move.

To Choose a Menu Command

1. In an application's menu bar, click the name of the menu that contains the command you want to choose. The corresponding menu list appears on the screen in front of the application window.

2. Click the command.

When you choose a menu command, the program immediately carries out the action that the command represents. Many menu commands are followed by ellipses (...) in Windows menus. This means that the command initially produces a *dialog box* in which you can supply specific instructions for carrying out the action.

To View a Control Menu

Click the control-menu box at the upper-left corner of the application window to view the application's control menu. (Look back at Figure 1.1 on page 4 to see the location of the control-menu box.)

 reminder

In many applications, each document window has its own control menu for carrying out operations related to the

12

document itself. The control-menu box for a document appears in the upper-left corner of the document window.

Using the Keyboard

Most Windows operations are easiest to perform with the mouse, but the keyboard occasionally provides useful short-cuts. Some computer users dislike having to lift their fingers off the keyboard to use the mouse; if you are this kind of user, you'll want to become familiar with at least a few of the Windows keyboard commands.

To Choose a Menu Command

1. Press the Alt key to activate the menu bar in the application you are currently using.

2. Press the shortcut key that represents the menu you want to view. This letter is underlined in each menu name displayed in the menu bar. (Alternatively, press the right- or left-arrow key repeatedly until the menu you want to see is highlighted, then press Enter.) This action displays the menu over the top of the application window.

3. Press the shortcut key for the command that you want to choose. (Or press the down- or up-arrow key repeat-edly until the command is highlighted, then press Enter.)

 tip

Suppose you decide not to choose any command from a menu you have pulled down. To return to your work in the application menu without choosing a command, press Esc twice—once to close the menu you have pulled down, and again to deactivate the menu bar.

To View a Control Menu

1. Press Alt to activate the menu bar in the active application.

2. Press the Spacebar to pull down the application's control menu, or press the hyphen key to pull down the control menu for the active document.

 reminder

See the following for some of the uses of the control menu: *Closing an Application* (page 19); *Minimizing, Maximizing, and Restoring a Window* (page 22); *Moving a Window* (page 24); *Sizing a Window* (page 26), and *Switching to Another Application* (page 15).

Running an Application

An application that is available for you to run is represented as an icon in one of the group windows of Program Manager. An application that is already running may be minimized—represented as an icon on the desktop. (See *Minimizing, Maximizing, and Restoring a Window* on page 22 for details.)

When you choose an application from Program Manager, Windows runs the application and opens its window so you can begin your work. When you choose an application icon from the desktop, the application's window is restored so you can continue your work.

To Start an Application

1. Switch to Program Manager.

2. If necessary, open the program group where the application's icon is displayed. (Double-click the group icon to open the window.)

3. Double-click the application icon to start the application and open its window onto the desktop.

To Open a Running Application

1. Move the mouse pointer over the application's icon on the desktop.

2. Double-click the left mouse button to open (or *restore*) the application window.

 reminder

You can also use the Run command in the Program Manager's File menu to start an application. See *Running an Application* in Part 2.

Switching to Another Application

⊚ ⊚ ⊚ ⊚ ⊚ ⊚ ⊚ ⊚ ⊚ ⊚ ⊚ ⊚ ⊚ ⊚ ⊚ ⊚ ⊚ ⊚ ⊚ ⊚

During a session with Windows, the icons and windows on the desktop represent all the applications that you are currently running. Things can get confusing when you have many windows open at once. Some windows may overlap with others, or one application window may completely hide all of the others. When this is the case, you need a quick way to switch from one application to another.

The Task List window is one convenient tool that you can use for this purpose. It shows you a list of all the applications you are currently running in Windows and allows you to switch easily to a new application. The Task List is available to you instantly at any time in your work.

 reminder

The *active* application window is the one in which you are currently working. Only one window is active at a time.

To Open the Task List and Switch to Another Application

1. Move the mouse pointer to any empty spot in the background of the desktop—that is, a place where there is no application window or icon.

2. Double-click the left mouse button. The Task List appears on the screen. The upper section of the Task List shows the names of all the applications currently running in Windows. (Figure 1.2 shows what the Task List looks like when several applications are running in Windows.)

3. Select the application that you want to switch to by clicking its name with the mouse.

4. Click the Switch To button to make the switch. The program you've selected becomes the active application.

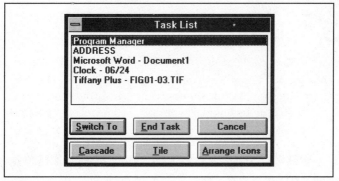

FIGURE 1.2: *The Task List*

 tip

If you change your mind, press Esc to close the Task List without switching to a different application.

 **shortcut**

If no part of the Windows background is visible, you can open the Task List by pressing Ctrl+Esc from the keyboard. From the keyboard, press the up- or down-arrow key repeatedly to highlight an application name from the Task List. Then press Enter to switch to the application you have selected.

Alternatively, press Alt and then Spacebar to open the control menu for the active application, and choose the Switch To command to open the Task List.

shortcut

Once the Task List is open, you can also double-click the name of an application—rather than clicking the Switch To button—to activate the application window. Another shortcut is to use the fast-switching technique, as described in the following steps.

To Switch Quickly from One Application to Another on the Desktop

1. Hold down the Alt key and press the Tab key. A rectangular box appears on the screen showing the name and icon of an application currently running in Windows.

2. Without releasing the Alt key, press the Tab key one or more additional times, until the name of the application that you want to switch to appears in the box.

3. Release the Alt key. The selected application becomes the active window.

 tip

If this technique does not work, someone has turned the fast-switching feature off in your installation of Windows. See the *Desktop Settings* entry in Part 5 of this book for instructions on turning fast swtiching back on again.

Closing an Application

A Windows application usually has an Exit command in its File menu. You can choose this command to close the application window. As a result, the window disappears from the desktop, and the application itself is no longer running.

 reminder

See *Using the Keyboard* on page 13 or *Using the Mouse* on page 9 for information about choosing menu commands.

Before you close an application, you typically need to decide whether or not to save the file or files you've been creating inside the application window. For example, if you're doing work in a word processor, you should save any documents you've created or changed before exiting. In many cases, an application will warn you that you have not saved a particular document and will give you a chance to save it before you close the application.

 a better way

Save each document *before* you choose the Exit command. You usually save documents within an application by choosing the Save command from the File menu.

To Exit an Application and Close its Window

1. Save any documents you've been working on in the application.

2. Pull down the File menu (by clicking the menu with the mouse or by pressing Alt and then F on the keyboard).

3. Choose the Exit command in the File menu list.

warning

Do not try to close the Program Manager window until you are ready to exit Windows. Program Manager always stays open during a given Windows session. When you close this particular window, you drop out of Windows and go back into DOS.

You can also use an application's control menu to close the window. This menu is represented by the small control-menu box located at the upper-left corner of an application window. For example, Figure 1.3 shows the control-menu box for the application named Clock. When you click this box, the control menu appears in the application window.

To Use the Control-Menu Box to Close an Application

1. Save any documents you've been working on in the application.

20

2. Click the control-menu box with the mouse (or press Alt and then Spacebar from the keyboard) to pull down the control menu.

3. Choose the Close command from the control menu.

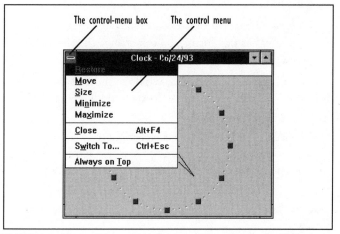

FIGURE 1.3: *The control menu and the control-menu box for the Clock*

 **shortcut**

The control menu provides two good shortcuts for closing an application. From the keyboard, press Alt+F4 (that is, hold down the Alt key and press the F4 key). Or, using the mouse, double-click the control-menu box.

 tip

If an application is minimized—that is, if it is represented on the desktop by its icon rather than a window—you can simply click the icon once to view the control menu.

Minimizing, Maximizing, and Restoring a Window

An application window can usually be arranged in any of three visual forms:

- A window that takes up less than the full screen. When a window has this form, you can change the size of the window and move it to any position on the screen.

- A full-screen, or *maximized*, window. In this form, the window takes up the entire desktop and hides any other applications currently open.

- An icon, representing a *minimized* application. In this form, the application is still running but is temporarily placed out of the way of your other work on the desktop.

 reminder

Note the distinction between *closing* an application window and *minimizing* it. When you close a window, the application is no longer running.

You can easily change a window to any of these three forms by using the minimize, maximize, and restore buttons that appear at the upper-right corner of a window. (Look back at Figure 1.1 on page 4 to see the location of the minimize and maximize buttons. When a window is maximized, the restore button takes the place of the maximize button.) Or you can pull down the window's control menu and choose the Restore, Minimize, or Maximize command to change the form of the active window.

tip

Some applications allow you to create and open multiple documents inside the application window. For example, Microsoft Word for Windows allows you to open as many as nine word-processed documents at a time, and Microsoft Excel allows you to open multiple worksheets, charts, and macro sheets. In this kind of application, each open document may have its own minimize, maximize, and restore buttons. Don't confuse these with the buttons that belong to the application window itself.

To Reduce a Window to Its Icon

1. Click the minimize button with the mouse. The application's window disappears and is replaced by an icon on the desktop.

2. Drag the icon to any convenient location on the desktop. (See *Using the Mouse* on page 9 for information about dragging an item.)

If you prefer to use the keyboard, press Alt and then Spacebar to view the control menu for the current window, and then press N to choose the Minimize command.

To View a Window in Its Full-Screen Size

Click the maximize button. When you do so, the window takes up the entire desktop and the maximize button changes to a restore button (with arrow heads pointing up and down).

To Maximize an Application That Currently Appears As an Icon on the Desktop

1. Click the icon once to view the application's control menu.

2. Choose the Maximize command from the control menu.

To Restore the Previous Size of a Maximized Window

Click the restore button at the far upper-right corner of the window. The window returns to the dimensions it had before you maximized it.

If you prefer to use the keyboard to restore the size of a window, press Alt and then Spacebar to pull down the control menu, and then press Enter to choose the first command in the menu, Restore.

Moving a Window

When a window takes up less than the full desktop (that is, when the window is *not* maximized), you can use the mouse or the keyboard to move the window to any convenient position on the screen. A maximized window cannot be moved.

To Move a Window with the Mouse

1. Move the mouse pointer anywhere within the title bar at the top of the window. (Look back at Figure 1.1 on page 4 to see the title bar in a window.)

2. Hold down the left mouse button and drag the window to a new position on the desktop. As you move the mouse, the window's new position is represented by a gray frame.

3. Release the mouse button to complete the move.

 tip

Before releasing the mouse button, you can cancel a move operation by pressing the Esc key on the keyboard. The gray window frame disappears, and the window itself stays in its original position. (Release the mouse button after you press Esc.)

To Move a Window with the Keyboard

1. Press Alt and then Spacebar to pull down the active window's control menu.

2. Press M to choose the Move command in the control menu. When you do so, the mouse pointer takes on a new shape: a cross with arrowheads pointing in four directions.

3. Press the up- or down-arrow key to move the window up or down in increments. Press the left- or right-arrow key to move the window horizontally in increments. As you do so, a light-gray frame represents the new position of the window.

4. When the gray frame is in the position where you want to move the window, press Enter. The window moves to its new position and the gray frame disappears.

 tip

You can cancel a move operation by pressing Esc instead of Enter.

Sizing a Window

When a window takes up less than the full desktop (that is, when the window is not maximized), you can use the mouse or the keyboard to change the window size on the desktop to any convenient dimensions. A maximized window cannot be resized.

To Size a Window with the Mouse

1. If the window is maximized, click the restore button.

2. To change the horizontal length of the window, position the mouse pointer over the window's left or right border. The mouse pointer becomes a double-headed arrow pointing left and right. Hold down the left mouse button and drag the border to increase or decrease the length. As you drag, a light-gray shadow indicates the new dimension of the window. Release the mouse button to confirm the new dimension.

3. To change the vertical height of the window, position the mouse pointer over the window's top or bottom border and drag the border to increase or decrease the height. Release the mouse button to confirm the new dimension.

4. To change two dimensions at once, position the mouse pointer over any of the window's four corners. The mouse pointer becomes a two-headed white arrow, pointing in diagonal directions. Drag diagonally to change both the height and the width at once. Release the mouse button to complete the resizing.

Before releasing the mouse button, you can cancel a resizing operation by pressing the Esc key on the keyboard.

To Size a Window with the Keyboard

1. Press Alt and then Spacebar to pull down the control menu of the active window.

2. Choose the Size command from the control menu. When you do so, the pointer moves to the center of the window and takes the shape of a cross with arrowheads pointing in four directions.

3. Press any combination of the up-, down-, left-, and right-arrow keys repeatedly. As you do so, a light-gray frame shows the window's new dimensions.

4. Press Enter to confirm the new dimensions. The window takes on its new size, and the light-gray frame disappears.

Moving Around in a Window

Because you may not be able to see all of a window's contents at once, *scroll bars* are available for moving to areas of the window that are not currently displayed. A window has scroll bars only if there is something to scroll to; if all of the window's contents can be seen within the current dimensions of the window, no scroll bars appear.

Depending upon the scrolling requirements of a given window, you might see a vertical scroll bar at the right side of the window, a horizontal scroll bar at the bottom of the window, or both. At either end of a scroll bar are small buttons with arrows—pointing up and down in a vertical scroll bar, or left and right in a horizontal scroll bar. Inside a scroll bar is a small *scroll box* that you can drag through the length of the bar.

To Scroll Vertically or Horizontally through the Contents of a Window

1. Click the up- or down-arrow button on the vertical scroll bar repeatedly to scroll up or down the window.

2. Click the left- or right-arrow button on the horizon tal scroll bar repeatedly to scroll left or right within the window.

 shortcut

Alternatively, you can drag the scroll box (up or down the vertical scroll bar, or left or right within the horizontal scroll bar) to scroll to a proportional location within the window's contents. For example, to scroll approximately halfway through the window's contents, drag the scroll box to the halfway point within the length of the scroll bar. You can also scroll up or down the windows by clicking above or below the scroll box.

reminder

You may see scroll bars both on an application window and on document windows within an application. The more information a window contains, the more important scroll bars become in your work.

Viewing Windows on the Desktop

One of the most attractive features of Windows is that you can not only run multiple applications at one time, but you can also view the windows of two or more applications side-by-side on the screen. You can arrange windows manually by moving and resizing them with the mouse, or you can use the Tile or Cascade button in the Task List window to display windows in a predefined arrangement.

To View Two or More Application Windows at the Same Time

1. If the active window is maximized, click its restore button to reduce it to its previous dimensions.

2. Minimize any windows that you do not want to include in the current desktop display.

3. Use the mouse or the keyboard to move and resize each of the remaining windows in the way you want to view them.

 reminder

See *Moving a Window* on page 24 and *Sizing a Window* on page 26 for mouse and keyboard techniques you can use to rearrange items on the desktop.

To View Windows
in a Cascade or Tile Arrangement

1. Minimize any applications that you do not want to include in the desktop arrangement, and restore the applications that you do want to include.

2. Double-click the mouse in a blank area of the desktop background (or press Ctrl+Esc) to open the Task List.

3. Click the Tile button in the Task List window to arrange the open windows in a side-by-side arrangement on the screen, or click Cascade to overlap the open windows in a stack, one in front of another.

Part 2

Program Manager

Introduction

The Program Manager window displays groups of application icons and gives you easy ways to choose the programs that you want to run. Program Manager is available on the desktop from the beginning to the end of a session with Windows. To exit Windows, you close the Program Manager window.

Initially, Program Manager may appear either as an icon or an open window on the desktop. If it appears as an icon, you simply double-click the icon to open the window. Inside the Program Manager window, you'll find icons that represent group windows. All the group icons look the same, but each is labeled with a description that tells you what kind of applications are in the group.

Double-click a group icon to open the group window. In the group window are individual icons (known as *program items*) representing the items in the group. A group can include both application icons and document icons. When you choose—or double-click—an application icon, Windows starts the application. When you choose a document icon, Windows starts the application in which the document was created and then opens the document itself.

Open the group called Main, and your Program Manager window will look approximately like Figure 2.1. As you can see, the Main group has a number of icons arranged in rows. Beneath the Main window are the icons for other groups.

When you first install Windows on your computer, the Setup program creates five groups in the Program Manager. These groups are named Main, Accessories, Games, Applications, and StartUp. Here's what these groups contain:

- The Main group provides programs known as *system applications*. Two important examples are File Manager and Control Panel. File Manager is designed to help you view and change the contents of your disks. Control Panel contains many options for modifying the way Windows works. You can learn about these and other system applications in Parts 3, 4, and 5 of this book.

- The Accessories group contains a useful set of applications that are packaged with Windows. Most notably, Write is a simple word-processing program, Paintbrush is a drawing program, and Cardfile is a program you can use to manage information such as addresses or employee records. Part 3 of this book shows you how to perform specific tasks in these and other Windows applications.

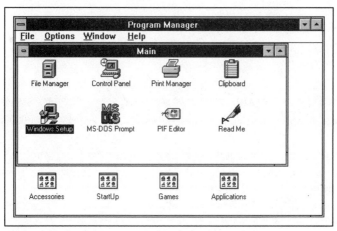

FIGURE 2.1: The Main group and other group icons

- The Games group presents beautifully designed—and appallingly addictive—entertainment programs for people who have lots of time on their hands.

- The Applications group contains icons for applications found on your hard disk at the time you installed Windows on your computer.

- The StartUp group is a special window; it is empty initially, but you can copy or move icons to it from other groups. The applications in the StartUp group are run automatically at the beginning of each session with Windows. See *Running an Application Automatically* on page 37 for more information.

Additional groups may appear in the Program Manager window when you install new Windows applications. For example, you might find groups named Word for Windows 2.0, Microsoft Excel 4.0, or Microsoft Access, if these particular applications are installed on your computer.

In the entries of Part 2, you'll learn to accomplish a variety of important tasks within the Program Manager window—such as running applications, creating new items and groups, arranging items that appear inside the Program Manager window, and getting help.

Running an Application

The most convenient way to run an application from Windows is to choose the icon that represents the application. The programs that you run on a daily basis should all be represented as icons in the various group windows of the Program Manager. (See *Creating a Program Item in a Group* on page 45 to learn how to add a new icon to a group.) But in some cases, there may be no group window and no icon for a program you want to run. In this case, you can use the Run command from the Program Manager's File menu to run the program.

To Run an Application That Is Represented by an Icon

1. In Program Manager, open the group window that contains the icon for the application you want to start.

2. Double-click the icon.

 tip

To choose an icon from the keyboard, press the right- or left-arrow key until the icon's caption is highlighted. Then press the Enter key to start the program that the icon represents. (To select a group, press Ctrl+Tab repeatedly until the group icon you want is highlighted, then press Enter to open the group window.)

To Use the Run Command

1. Click the File menu in the Program Manager's menu bar (or press Alt and then F to pull down the menu).

2. Choose the Run command in the menu. The Run dialog box appears on the screen, as shown in Figure 2.2. (The dialog box includes a Command Line *text box* in which you can type the name of the program you want to run; a *check box* labeled Run Minimized that you can use to specify whether the application will appear as an icon or a window on the desktop when it starts; and a column of four *command buttons* that you can choose to carry out the various operations of the Run command.)

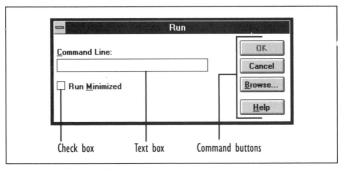

Check box   Text box   Command buttons

FIGURE 2.2: *The Run dialog box*

3. Enter the path and file name of the application that you
want to run. (In the *path*, you identify the disk and directory location of the file. For example, *c:\apps\address*
identifies a program named *address* in a directory named
apps on drive C.)

4. If you want the program to be minimized as an icon
when it starts, click the Run Minimized check box. An X
appears in the box. (If you want the program to appear as
a window when it starts, leave this box unchecked.)

5. Click the OK button (or press Enter from the keyboard)
to start the program.

 tip

If you can't remember where the file for a particular program
is located on your hard disk, click the Browse button on the
Run dialog box (or press Alt+B from the keyboard). The resulting Browse dialog box provides a list of the directories on
your disk, and a list of the program files in a selected directory. To view the programs in a particular directory, double-
click the directory's name in the directory list. To select a

36

program file, click its name in the file list. Then click OK to close the Browse dialog box. The file's complete name and path then appears in the Command Line text box of the Run dialog box.

Running an Application Automatically

If there are some programs that you want to run automatically in Windows, you can copy or move their icons to the StartUp group in Program Manager. In response, these applications are opened onto the desktop at the beginning of each session with Windows.

To Copy a Program Icon to the StartUp Group

1. In the Program Manager window, open the group window that contains the program icon you want to copy to the StartUp group.

2. Hold down the Ctrl key and drag the icon from the open group window to the StartUp group. (The StartUp group need not be open; if it is not, drag the program icon onto the StartUp group icon.)

3. Release the mouse button and the Ctrl key.

reminder

You can also use the Copy command in the File menu to copy an application icon. See *Copying a Program Item to a Group* on page 49 for more information about this task.

a better way

Copying an icon to the StartUp group is generally a better idea than moving the icon to StartUp. If you move an icon, the icon's original group window no longer contains a copy of the icon. See *Moving a Program Item to a Group* on page 47 for more information. If the icon you want to place in the StartUp group does not yet exist in any of the current group windows, you can create a new icon in StartUp. See *Creating a Program Item in a Group* on page 45.

Creating a New Group Window

To improve the convenience of the Program Manager window, you might sometimes want to create a new group window for a particular group of application icons. For example, suppose you typically use your word-processing program, a spreadsheet program, and File Manager during most day-to-day activities in Windows. To avoid having to open up three different group windows to start these three programs, you can copy their icons to a single window. You might give the window a simple name like Daily, because it contains the programs that you use every day.

To Use the New Command

1. Pull down the File menu in the Program Manager menu bar.

2. Choose the New command. The resulting dialog box contains two *option buttons*, Program Group and Program Item. (Only one of these options can be selected at a time.)

3. If the Program Group option is not already selected, click the option button with the mouse or press Alt+G from the keyboard.

4. Click the OK button, or press Enter. A new dialog box named Program Group Properties appears on the screen.

5. In the Description text box, enter the name that you want displayed in the title bar of the new group window. You may leave the second text box, labeled Group File, blank.

6. Click OK or press Enter to complete the operation. Windows creates the new group window and displays it inside the Program Manager window.

techno note

Windows creates a file on disk to record the properties of each group window that appears in the Program Manager window. The extension name for group files is GRP. For example, if you create a new group named Daily, Windows creates a group file named DAILY.GRP. If you wish, you can specify the name for the group file by entering a file name into the Group File text box in the Program Group Properties dialog box.

reminder

Once you create a new group window, you can copy or move icons to the window from existing groups, or you can create new icons in the window. See *Creating a Program Item in a Group* (page 45), *Moving a Program Item to a Group* (page 47), and *Copying a Program Item to a Group* (page 49) for details.

Arranging Group Windows

You can arrange the group windows in Program Manager in any way that simplifies your typical daily activities in Windows. Only one group is *active* at a time; the active group is the one that responds to your choices. But you can open any number of group windows so that you can see the application icons they contain. For example, you might want to keep open the group windows that include the applications you use most often. You can open other group windows when you need to run applications they contain.

 reminder

The mouse and keyboard techniques for moving and sizing group windows are similar to those for arranging windows on the desktop. (See the *Moving a Window* and *Sizing a Window* entries in Part 1 for more details.)

tip

Of course, the arrangement of group windows is limited by the current size of the Program Manager window itself. You cannot move or resize a group window outside the border of the Program Manager. To give yourself the largest possible space to arrange your work in, you can maximize the Program Manager window.

To Move and Resize a Group Window with the Mouse

1. If the group window is not yet open, double click its icon to open it.

2. Drag the group window by its title bar to move it to a new position within the Program Manager window.

3. Drag any of the group window's four borders—top, bottom, left or right—or any of its four corners to increase or decrease the dimensions of the window.

 note

Some application groups contain a main program icon along with several other icons that represent programs or documents related to the application. For convenience, you can reduce the size of group windows and arrange their icons so that only one program icon is displayed. For example, Figure 2.3 shows a Program Manager window with several small group windows displaying one program icon each.

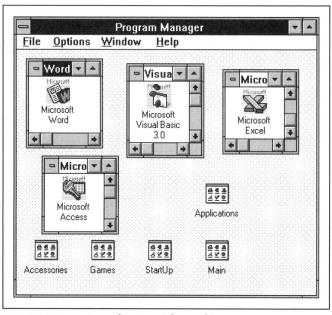

FIGURE 2.3: *Arranging application windows and icons*

To Move and Resize a Group Window from the Keyboard

1. Press Ctrl+Tab repeatedly until the group you want to change becomes active.

2. If the group appears as an icon, press Enter to open the group window.

3. Press Alt+− (Alt+hyphen) to view the control menu for the active group window.

4. Choose the Move command from the control menu, then press any combination of up-, down-, right-, and left-arrow keys to move the window to a new position within the Program Manager window. Press Enter to confirm the move.

5. Press Alt+– (Alt+hyphen) and then choose the Size command from the control menu. Use arrow keys to increase or decrease the window's dimensions, and then press Enter to confirm.

To View Group Windows in a Cascade or Tile Arrangement

1. Open all the group windows that you want to include in the cascade or tile arrangement.

2. Pull down the Window menu from the Program Manager's menu bar. Choose Cascade to view the open groups as a stack of overlapping windows, or choose Tile to view the windows side-by-side.

shortcut

You can use keyboard shortcuts to rearrange the open group windows: Shift+F5 for the Cascade command, or Shift+F4 for the Tile command.

tip

Unopened groups—appearing as icons in the Program Manager window—are not affected by the Cascade and Tile commands.

Arranging Icons

You can rearrange the group icons in the Program Manager window and the application icons in a given group window in any way you want. You can also choose between a free-form arrangement or a regular arrangement in rows and columns.

To arrange icons manually

1. Activate and open the Program Manager window, or the group window in which you want to rearrange icons.

2. Use the mouse to drag each icon to a suitable position.

 warning

When you begin the process of dragging an application icon from one position to another, be careful to select the icon with a single click, not a double click. A double click will start the program.

To Arrange Icons in Regular Rows or Columns

1. Activate and open the Program Manager window, or the group window in which you want to rearrange the icons. (If you want to arrange group icons in the Program Manager window, minimize all the group windows that you want to include in the new arrangement.)

2. Pull down the Window menu from the Program Manager menu bar and choose the Arrange Icons command. In response, Windows arranges the icons in rows and columns within the current dimensions of the active window.

To arrange icons automatically

1. Pull down the Options menu from the Program Manager menu bar.

2. If the Auto Arrange command does not already have a check mark (✓) next to it, choose the command. (If a check mark is already displayed, press Esc twice to close the menu without choosing a command.)

3. Resize the Program Manager window or any of the group windows. When you do so, Windows automatically rearranges the icons in the window to fit within the new dimensions.

Creating a Program Item in a Group

Suppose your hard disk contains an application that is not yet represented as an icon in any of the group windows of Program Manager. You can use the New command in the File menu to create an icon for the program in any group of your choice.

To Add a Program Item Using the New Command

1. Activate and open the group in which you want to add the new program icon.

2. Pull down the File menu in the Program Manager menu bar and choose the New command. In the resulting New Program Object dialog box, the Program Item option is selected.

3. Without changing the selection, click the OK button or press Enter. The Program Item Properties dialog box appears on the screen.

4. In the Description text box, enter the caption that you want to appear beneath the program icon.

5. In the Command Line text box, enter the path and file name for the program that the icon will represent.

6. Click OK or press Enter. The new icon appears in the active group window.

techno note

The Program Item Properties dialog box has some optional items. For example, you can enter a directory into the Working Directory text box in the Program Item Properties box. This will become the default directory for files that you save from the application. In the Shortcut Key text box, you can define a keyboard sequence that starts the application or activates it when it is already running. (See *Setting the Properties of a Program Item* on page 50 for more information.)

tip

If you don't know the directory location of the program that you want to add to the active group window, click the Browse button on the Program Item Properties dialog box. Use the directory list and the file list in the resulting Browse dialog box to locate and select the program file. (See *Running an Application* on page 34 for more information about the Browse feature.)

Moving a Program Item to a Group

When you move a program item, the icon disappears from its original group and goes to a different group. You might want move an icon in order to place it in a more convenient location in the Program Manager window.

You can move an icon either by dragging it with the mouse or by choosing the Move command from the Program Manager's File menu.

 reminder

Note the difference between moving a program item and copying an item. When you copy an icon, the icon remains in its original group and appears also in a second group. In this case, both the original and the copy represent the same program. See *Copying a Program Item to a Group* on page 49 for details.

To Move a Program Icon with the Mouse

1. Open the group where the icon is currently located.

2. Drag the icon to the group where you want it to appear.

 tip

The destination group need not be open. You can drag a program icon either to a group icon or to a group window to move the icon from one group to another.

To Use the Move Command

1. Open the group where the icon you want to move is currently located.

2. Select the program icon by clicking it once with the mouse.

3. Pull down the File menu and choose the Move command (or press F7 from the keyboard). The Move Program Item dialog box appears on the screen. The first two lines in the box identify the program item you have selected and the group from which you are moving it.

4. In the To Group box, select the group to which you want to move the program item. (Click the down-arrow button at the right side of the box to view a list of all the groups in the Program Manager window.)

5. Click OK or press Enter to complete the move operation.

Copying a Program Item to a Group

Sometimes you may find it convenient to have copies of a particular application icon in more than one group. All the copies represent the same program, and choosing any one of them will start the program. But the multiple copies allow you to start the program from more than one group.

To Copy a Program Icon with the Mouse

1. Open the group window that currently contains the program icon that you want to copy.

2. Hold down the Ctrl key on the keyboard.

3. Drag the program item to the group icon or group window where you want to copy the icon.

4. Release the mouse button and the Ctrl key.

5. Open the destination group window to make sure that the copy operation was successful. You should find a copy of the icon in the window.

 reminder

One common reason for copying a program item is to place the icon in the StartUp group. See *Running an Application Automatically* on page 37 for details.

49

 **technical**

The copy operation has no effect on the actual program file that is stored on disk; a second copy of the file is *not* created.

To Use the Copy Command

1. Open the group window that contains the program item that you want to copy.

2. Select the icon by clicking it once with the mouse.

3. Pull down the File menu and choose the Copy command (or press F8 from the keyboard). The Copy Program Item dialog box appears on the screen. The first two lines of the box identify the program item you have selected and the items current group window location.

4. In the To Group box, select the group to which you want to copy the program item. (Click the down-arrow button at the right side of the box to view a list of all the groups in the Program Manager window.)

5. Click OK or press Enter to complete the copy operation.

Setting the Properties
of a Program Item

Using the Properties command in the Program Manager's File menu, you can change several characteristics of a program item in a group window. For example, you can identify a document that will be opened whenever you start the application; you can create a shortcut key for activating the program; and you can change the icon that represents the program.

 tip

When you use the Properties command, the changes that you define apply only to one copy of the active program item. You can therefore create multiple copies of a program item with differently defined properties. For example, one copy of the item might be designed only to start a particular application, while another copy might start the application *and* open a document. (See *Copying a Program Item to a Group* on page 49 for information about making copies of an item.)

To Open a Document Automatically When You Run a Program

1. Open the group window containing the icon that represents the program.

2. Click the icon once to select it.

3. Pull down the File menu in the Program Manager's menu bar, and choose the Properties command (or simply press Alt+Enter from the keyboard). The Program Item Properties dialog box appears on the screen.

4. Activate the Command Line text box (by clicking inside the box, or by pressing Alt+C), and then press the End key to move the *insertion point* to the end of the file name displayed in the box. (The insertion point is a cursor that appears as a flashing vertical line.)

5. Press the Spacebar once, and then type the path and file name of the document that you want to open along with the application.

6. Click OK or press Enter to confirm this property change.

 tip

Suppose you want to open your AUTOEXEC.BAT file each time you choose the icon that represents the Notepad application. To arrange this, select the Notepad icon in the Accessories group, choose the Properties command from the File menu, and enter the name of the file just after NOTEPAD.EXE in the Command Line text box. When you are finished, the contents of the text box will appear as follows:

```
NOTEPAD.EXE \AUTOEXEC.BAT
```

Click OK to confirm. The AUTOEXEC.BAT file will be opened each time you start the application.

To Create a Shortcut Key For Running or Activating a Program

1. Open the group window that contains the program icon, and click the icon to select it.

2. Choose the Properties command from the File menu or press Alt+Enter.

3. In the Program Item Properties dialog box, activate the Shortcut Key text box by clicking inside the box with the mouse or by pressing Alt+S.

4. Press a keyboard combination in any one of these patterns: Ctrl+Alt+*character*, Ctrl+Shift+*character*, or Ctrl+Shift+Alt+*character* (where *character* is a letter, digit, or special character on the keyboard). The combination appears in the Shortcut Key box.

5. Click OK or press Enter to confirm.

 shortcut

When you define a shortcut key combination, you can use it to start an application or to activate an application that is already running.

To Change the Icon that Represents a Program

1. Open the group window that contains the program icon, and click the icon once to select it.

2. Choose the Properties command from the File menu, or press Alt+Enter.

3. In the Program Item Properties dialog box, click the Change Icon button. The Change Icon dialog box appears on the screen.

4. Type **C:\WINDOWS\PROGMAN.EXE** in the File Name text box and press Enter. In response, the Current Icon box displays a large collection of icons that you can choose from for any program item.

5. Scroll horizontally through the collection of icons until you find the one that you want. Select it and then click OK to confirm and to close the Change Icon dialog box.

6. Click OK again in the Program Item Properties dialog box to make the change.

 note

If you create duplicate program items for starting a particular application in different ways, you may want to change the icon for one or more of the items. For example, you might want to replace an application icon with an icon depicting a document that is opened automatically when you start the program.

Deleting Icons
and Group Windows

You can delete any group window or program item from Program Manager. This may simplify the organization of the Program Manager window, especially if there are groups or items that you never use.

 reminder

Deleting a program item from a group does not delete the program file itself from disk. The program itself is still available, even though it is no longer represented by an icon in the Program Manager.

To Delete an Icon Using the Delete Command

1. Open the group window that contains the program item you want to delete. Select the item by clicking it once with the mouse.

2. Pull down the File menu and choose the Delete command (or simply press the Del key on the keyboard). A warning box appears on the screen, asking you to confirm the deletion.

3. Click the Yes button to carry out the deletion. (Click No if you change your mind.) The program item disappears from the group window.

To Delete a Group Window Using the Delete Command

1. Close the group window that you want to delete, and then select the group icon. (If you select a group icon by clicking it with the mosue, you'll need to click again to close the pop-up control menu.)

2. Choose the Delete command from the File menu, or press Del from the keyboard.

3. Click the Yes button in the warning box to confirm the deletion.

warning

When you delete a group window, all of the program items in the window are deleted at once. If you want to delete only a selection of program items, open the window and delete the icons one at a time.

Getting Help

Windows has an elaborate and flexible on-line help system that provides you with a vast amount of information about Windows operations and applications. This system is an application by itself and always appears in its own window. There are several ways to start the Help system and find the information that you need.

To Open Program Manager Help

1. Pull down the Help menu and choose the Contents command. The Program Manager Help window appears on the screen with a list of general topics you can read about.

2. Click any underlined selection to go immediately to a particular topic.

 note

You can return to the general list of contents by clicking the Contents button at the top of the Help window.

 shortcut

Press the F1 function key to open the Help window at any time during your work in Windows. Whenever possible,

Windows opens a help topic related to your current activity. This is known as *context-sensitive* help.

To Find Information about a Specific Feature

1. Pull down the Help menu and choose the Search for Help on command. The Search window appears on the screen.

2. In the text box near the top of the window, type the word or words that identify the topic you want to search for, and click the Show Topics button or press Enter. (Alternatively, select a topic in the list box that appears in the upper half of the Search Window.)

3. In the list box at the bottom of the dialog box, select the topic you want to read about, and click the Go To button. The Help window appears on the screen, displaying the help topic that you requested.

shortcut

You can open the Search dialog box directly from the Help window. Simply click the Search button that appears at the top of the Help window.

To Run the Windows Tutorial

Pull down the Help menu and choose the Windows Tutorial command. Follow the instructions that appear on the screen for running the tutorial.

tip

The Windows Tutorial is an important way to learn basic information about Windows operations. You should go through the entire Tutorial at least once while you are first learning to use Windows.

To Get Information about Program Manager and the Windows Mode

Pull down the Help menu and choose the About Program Manager command. The resulting dialog box shows you the version number, the mode (standard or enhanced), and the amount of memory available. Click OK to close the window.

Part 3

Applications That Come with Windows

● ● ● ● ● ● ● ● ● ● ● ● ● ● ● ● ● ● ●

Introduction

Windows comes with a collection of applications in which you can create documents, save and retrieve information, and do several other kinds of work. For example, Windows gives you a nuts-and-bolts word-processing program named Write, a data file–management program named Cardfile, and an amusing and useful drawing program named Paintbrush. You'll find the icons for these and other applications in the Accessories group of the Program Manager window. These programs are simple to use. They do not provide the power and flexibility—nor the complexity—of major applications like Word for Windows or Microsoft Access. But they come free with Windows, and they are more than adequate for many day-to-day computer tasks.

In addition, Windows supplies a variety of system applications—sometimes known as utilities—designed to help you use the hardware and software resources of your computer. Among these are Print Manager, File Manager, Clipboard, and Control Panel.

Part 3 gives instructions for carrying out basic tasks in a selection of these Windows applications and utilities. (Part 4 covers the File Manager, and Part 5 introduces the features of the Control Panel.) Once you've mastered your first few Windows applications, you'll find that new programs take you less and less time to learn. All major Windows applications display on the screen similar types of objects—such as menus, icons, document windows, scroll bars, and dialog boxes. In addition, Windows applications recognize familiar mouse and keyboard operations, and make use of your computer's components in parallel ways.

Calendar

⦿ ⦿

The Calendar application gives you a convenient way to keep track of daily appointments for any date on your business or social calendar. When you first start Calendar, it shows an appointment sheet for the current date; this is called the day view. You can also switch to the month view for a one-month calendar display.

To Start a New Calendar File

1. Open the Accessories group in the Program Manager, and double-click the Calendar icon. The application window opens with today's appointment sheet.

2. Choose the Save As command from the File menu to create a file for your personal appointments.

3. In the Save As dialog box, enter a file name for your calendar. The application automatically adds CAL as the extension name for the file.

4. Click OK.

 tip

Give your calendar a file name that clearly identifies it as your personal appointment record. For example, use your first name, your last name, or your initials as the name for the file. Then other people who also use the Calendar application on the same computer will not inadvertantly record their appointments in your file.

To Select a Date for Viewing or Recording an Appointment

1. Pull down the View menu from the Calendar menu bar and choose Month. This switches you to the month view; a display of the current month appears in the Calendar window.

2. If the appointment you want to view or record is not in the current month, click one of the two scroll arrows that appear just above the month's calendar. Each click moves you one month backward or forward in time.

3. When you reach the month in which you want to view or record an appointment, double-click the date that you want to open. In response, Calendar switches you to the day view, where you can see any appointments that you have recorded previously, or you can record a new appointment.

 tip

There are several other ways to switch to a new date in the Calendar:

- To scroll to a new date in day view, click either of the scroll arrows that appear at the top of the appointment sheet. Each click moves you one day backward or forward.

- Pull down the Show menu and choose Today to bring up today's appointments; or choose Previous or Next to move backward or forward by a day.

- Choose Date from the Show menu. In the Show Date dialog box, enter the date that you want to switch to.

The appointment sheet for that date appears in the Calendar window.

shortcut

To switch quickly from the day view to the month view, press the F9 function key or double-click the date at the top of the appointment sheet.

To Record an Appointment in the Calendar

1. Select the date in which you want to record the appointment, and switch to the day view.

2. If the time for the appointment is not visible in the appointment sheet, use the scroll bars to scroll up or down the sheet.

3. Click the time for the appointment. A flashing insertion point appears to the right of the time entry.

4. Type the text of your appointment. You may type up to 80 characters in the appointment description.

note

At the bottom of the appointment sheet is a small scratch-pad area in which you can type brief notes that apply to the current day—for example, "Elaine's birthday," or "Pay quarterly taxes today." To make an entry in the scratch pad, click the mouse inside the area and then type the text of your note.

To Open an Existing Calendar Document

1. Pull down the File menu and choose Open.

2. In the file list, select the name of the calendar file that you want to open.

3. Click OK.

 tip

If you want to open a calendar file without making any changes in it, click the Read Only option in the Open dialog box, then click OK.

Cardfile

Cardfile is a simple data-management application. It is ideal for storing addresses, employee lists, product descriptions, and other records of information that you need to be able to look up quickly and efficiently.

Each record of information that you store in a file is displayed in a rectangular "card" in the Cardfile window. The first line of each card is called the *index line*. Cardfile arranges the cards in a file in alphabetical order by the information you enter into the index line. Beneath a card's index line is the information area, where you can enter lines of text for each card. The front card in the file is the current record—that is, the card in which you can view and edit the contents of the information area. As you'll learn, Cardfile gives you several ways to bring a particular card to the front of the file for viewing and editing.

Probably the most common card file example is an address

file, where you enter a person's name on the index line of each card and the person's address and phone number in the description area. But card files don't always have to be strictly business related. For example, Figure 3.1 shows a bird watcher's card file. This particular illustration contains descriptions of birds commonly sighted in an urban setting. Each bird's common name is displayed on the index line of a given card. The information area provides the scientific name, followed by a brief description of the bird's habitat.

To Create a New Card File

1. Open the Accessories group in the Program Manager window, and double-click the Cardfile icon. The Cardfile window opens onto the desktop, and initially displays one blank card. The unsaved card file is identified as (Untitled).

2. Fill in the index line and description area of the first card. (See To Fill in the First Blank Card on page 66 for details.)

3. Pull down the Card menu and choose Add for each new card you want to add to the file. (See To Add a New Card to the File on page 67 for details.)

4. Choose the Save As command from the File menu to save your card file. Enter a file name; Cardfile supplies the extension CRD.

 reminder

To open an existing card file, choose the Open command from the File menu and choose the name of the file you want to open. To close the current card file and start a new one, choose New from the File menu. To exit Cardfile, choose Exit from the File menu, or double-click the control-menu box at the upper-left corner of the application window.

FIGURE 3.1: *A bird-watcher's card file*

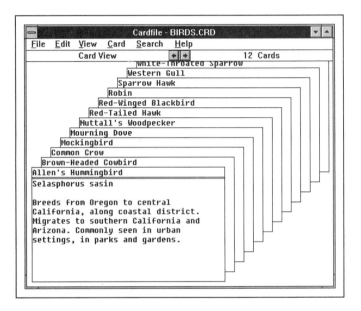

To Fill in the First Blank Card

1. Pull down the Edit menu and choose the Index command.

2. In the resulting Index dialog box, enter the text for the first card's index line. Then click OK to confirm. The text is copied to the card's index line, and the insertion point appears inside the information area.

3. Type the information you want to store on this first card.

shortcut

There are two shortcuts for opening the Index dialog box for a card: Double-click the card's index line, or select the card and press F6. You can use these techniques to enter the initial index text or to revise the index for an existing card.

tip

Word-wrap takes place when you reach the end of each line within the card: The insertion point automatically drops down to the beginning of the next line. Press the Enter key if you want to force a new line. (See the *Write* entry on page 84 for more information about the terms *word-wrap* and *insertion point*.)

To Add a New Card to the File

1. Pull down the Card menu and choose Add.

2. In the resulting Add dialog box, enter the text for the index line of the new card. Then click OK. Cardfile creates a new card and copies the text to the index line. The insertion point appears in the information area of the new card.

3. Type the information that you want to store in this card.

Cardfile automatically arranges your cards in alphabetical order by the text you have entered into the index lines.

To Change the View of the Cards

Pull down the View menu and choose the List command. In the resulting list view, you see an alphabetized list of the index lines of all your cards.

To change back to the card view, pull down the View menu and choose Card.

To Find a Specific Card

1. Pull down the Search menu and choose the Go To command. The Go To dialog box appears on the screen.

2. In the Go To text box, enter any part of the index line from the card that you want to find.

3. Click OK. Cardfile locates the card identified by your entry and brings it to the front of the card file. You can now view or edit the information in the card.

 tip

You don't have to enter the entire contents of an index line into the Go To dialog box. Enter any portion of the index text that uniquely identifies the card that you want to find. For example, to find the card with the name Mary Huntington, you can simply enter Hunt. As long as no other card has that string of characters in its index, Mary Huntington's card will come to the front. (If there are multiple cards containing Hunt in their index text, the next matching card will come to the front.)

 shortcut

The F4 function key is the shortcut for the Go To command. When you press F4, Cardfile immediately displays the Go To dialog box.

tip

Another way to bring a card to the front is simply to click its index line once with the mouse. From the keyboard, you can scroll through cards one at a time by pressing the PgUp or PgDn key.

To Find Text in the Information Area of a Card

1. Pull down the Search menu and choose Find. The Find dialog box appears on the screen.

2. In the Find What text box, enter the text that you want to find. (Keep in mind that Cardfile will search only in the information areas of cards for this text, not in the index lines.)

3. Click the Find Next button. Cardfile brings to the front the first card that contains the target text.

4. Repeat step 3 one or more times to search for the next occurrences of the same target text.

5. Click Cancel to close the Find dialog box.

 tip

Once the Find dialog box is closed, you can click F3 to repeat the search for the next occurrence of the target text.

To Edit the Index Line
of an Existing Card

1. Click the card's index line to bring the card to the front.

2. Choose the Index command from the Edit menu.

3. In the resulting dialog box, enter the new text that you want to display in the index line of the current card.

4. Click OK to confirm the change.

 shortcut

Press F6 to open the Index dialog box for the current card, or double-click the index line of the current card.

 warning

Keep in mind that Cardfile alphabetizes the cards in the file by their index lines. If you change the index line of a particular card, the card may be moved to a new place in the order of cards.

To Print a Card in the File

1. Select the card that you want to print, and bring it to the front of the file.

2. Pull down the File menu and choose the Print command.

To Print the Entire File

Pull down the File menu and choose the Print All command.

Clipboard

The Clipboard is a temporary storage place for information
that you are copying or moving from one place to another in
Windows. You can use the Clipboard for transfering text,
graphics, and combinations of both. You can copy or move
information within a single application, or from one application to another. Although you never have to open the Clipboard
to carry out a successful transfer of information, you can view
the contents of the Clipboard whenever you want to.

To Copy Information to the Clipboard

1. Start an application and open the document from which
you want to move or copy information.

2. Select the information that you want to transfer.

3. Pull down the application's Edit menu and choose the Cut
command for a move operation, or the Copy command
for a copy operation. In response, Windows transfers
the information to the Clipboard. (If you choose Cut,
the information disappears from the current document;
if you choose Copy, the information stays in place.)

shortcut

In most applications, you can press Ctrl+X to perform the Cut
command, or Ctrl+C to perform the Copy command.

To View the Contents of the Clipboard

1. Open the Main group in the Program Manager window.

2. Double-click the Clipboard icon. The Clipboard Viewer window shows the text and/or graphics that you most recently transferred to the Clipboard.

To Paste Information from the Clipboard

1. Start an application and open the document to which you want to move or copy information.

2. Move the cursor to the position where you want to display the transferred information.

3. Pull down the application's Edit menu and choose the Paste command. In response, Windows transfers the information from the Clipboard to the application.

 shortcut

In most applications, you can press Ctrl+V to perform the Paste command.

 tip

Pasting information from the Clipboard does not clear the Clipboard. If you want to paste a second copy of the information at some other location, you can simply choose the Paste command again. The same information remains in the Clipboard until you perform another Cut or Copy command.

MS-DOS Prompt

The MS-DOS Prompt utility allows you to run DOS programs from Windows, and then to return to your work in Windows when you are ready.

To Run DOS Programs from Windows

1. Open the Main group in the Program Manager window.

2. Double-click the MS-DOS Prompt icon. Windows disappears, and the DOS prompt appears on the screen.

3. Enter the DOS commands that you want to use.

warning

Avoid using the CHKDSK and UNDELETE commands while you are running a DOS session from Windows.

To Return to Windows

Type **exit** from the DOS prompt. Windows reappears on the screen, with the same applications running as when you left.

Notepad

The Notepad application is for creating or viewing text files. A text file consists of one or more lines of readable text, with no special application-specific formatting information. (You can view any text file from DOS by using the TYPE command.)

Notepad is a *text editor*, not a *word processor*. To read about the features of word processing, see the entry on Write on page 84.

To Create and Save a Notepad Document

1. Open the Accessories group in the Program Manager window, and double-click the icon for the Notepad application. The Notepad window that appears contains a blank work area for entering text.

2. Type the text that you want to save in the file. Press Enter at the end of each line.

3. Pull down the File menu and choose Save As.

4. In the Save As dialog box, enter a name for the file you are creating. By default, Notepad adds TXT as the file's extension name.

5. Click OK.

 tip

To include the current time and date in the text of your file, pull down the Edit menu and choose the Time/Date command.

 **techno note**

You can use the Notepad application to view or modify system files such as AUTOEXEC.BAT or CONFIG.SYS. (But don't make changes in these files unless you're sure you understand what the result will be.)

To Open a Text File

1. Choose the Open command from the File menu.

2. Select the file you want to open from the file list, or type its name directly into the File Name box.

3. Click OK.

To Print a Notepad Document

1. Open the file that you want to print.

2. Choose Print from the File menu.

Paintbrush

⊚ ⊚ ⊚ ⊚ ⊚ ⊚ ⊚ ⊚ ⊚ ⊚ ⊚ ⊚ ⊚ ⊚ ⊚ ⊚ ⊚ ⊚ ⊚ ⊚

In the Paintbrush application, you can create color or black-and-white pictures, using a variety of flexible drawing tools. Although it's possible to work in Paintbrush from the keyboard, the mouse is far more useful and efficient. Paintbrush makes distinct uses of both the left and the right mouse buttons.

The Paintbrush window includes several items:

⊚ A toolbox, at the left side of the window (see Figure 3.2). The toolbox displays icons representing the various drawing tools available in the application.

⊚ A linesize box, at the lower-left corner of the window. This box gives you a range of drawing widths to choose from.

⊚ A palette, shown along the bottom of the window. The Palette displays the colors or patterns you can use for the foreground and background of the pictures you draw.

⊚ The drawing area, taking up most of the window. This is where you draw your picture. Inside the drawing area, the mouse pointer (or cursor) shows the current position in your drawing. This pointer takes on different shapes for the different drawing tools you choose.

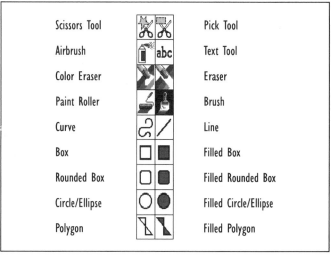

Scissors Tool		Pick Tool
Airbrush		Text Tool
Color Eraser		Eraser
Paint Roller		Brush
Curve		Line
Box		Filled Box
Rounded Box		Filled Rounded Box
Circle/Ellipse		Filled Circle/Ellipse
Polygon		Filled Polygon

FIGURE 3.2: *The Paintbrush toolbox*

In addition, Paintbrush has a menu bar with a variety of commands that relate to your work in the drawing area.

To Create a Drawing

1. Open the Accessories group in the Program Manager window, and double-click the Paintbrush icon. The Paintbrush application window opens onto the screen. Maximize the window to give yourself as much room as possible in which to work on your drawing.

2. Select a drawing color and, optionally, a new background color from the palette. (See *To Select Colors* on page 79 for detailed instructions.)

3. Select a drawing width from the linesize box. (See *To Select a Line Width* on page 80 for instructions.)

4. Select a drawing tool from the toolbox.

5. Move the mouse pointer into the drawing area, and drag the mouse to create elements of your drawing.

6. Repeat steps 3, 4, and 5 to create additional elements of your drawing.

7. Choose the Save As command from the File menu to save your drawing to disk. (See *To Save a Drawing* on page 82 for details.)

8. Choose Print from the File menu to print your drawing onto paper. (See *To Print a Drawing* on page 83.)

 a better way

The best way to learn to use Paintbrush is to experiment with it. Try using all the drawing tools, even before you've read anything about them. For the most part, it's easy to figure out how they work. You can create lots of experimental drawings without saving them or printing them. To erase your current drawing and start again with an empty drawing area, choose the New command from the File menu, or double-click the eraser tool. (Paintbrush displays a dialog box asking you whether you want to save the current drawing. As long as you're just experimenting, click the No button.)

tip

As shown in Figure 3.2, the toolbox has several categories of drawing tools. Here is a brief summary of what they do:

- The first two tools, Scissors and Pick, are also known as the *cutout tools*. You use them to enclose a part of your picture that you want to change in some way. Use the Scissors tool to define a free-form cutout of any shape, or the Pick tool to define a rectangular cutout. After defining a cutout, you can easily move, copy, or change the contents of the enclosed area. (See *To Define and Edit a Cutout* on page 81 for details.)

- Airbrush and Brush are the two major freehand drawing tools. As you drag the mouse through the drawing area, Airbrush gives a spray of dots, and Brush provides a solid line of color. Both tools draw in a variety of widths, as defined by your selection in the linesize box. The Brush tool can draw in a variety of shapes. (Double-click the Brush tool in the toolbox to view the Brush Shapes dialog box.) To draw straight lines with either of these tools, hold down the Shift key as you drag the mouse through the drawing area.

- The Text tool allows you incorporate text in your drawing. (See *To Add Text to a Drawing* on page 80 for details.)

- The Paint Roller fills the interior of an enclosed space with the current foreground color. To use this tool, you simply select a color, click the Paint Roller icon in the toolbox, and then click inside any space in the drawing area that is enclosed by a drawn border.

- The Color Eraser and the Eraser tools are designed to replace selections with another color. The Eraser replaces existing parts of your drawing with the current foreground color. The Color Eraser replaces instances of the foreground color with the background color that you select. You can increase or decrease the size of the eraser path by selecting a drawing width from the line-size box.

⊚ The remaining tools, in the bottom five rows of the toolbox, produces geometric shapes of various types, including curves, lines, rectangles, circles, and polygons. Enclosed shapes can be filled with the selected foreground color or unfilled, depending on the tool you select.

To Select Colors

1. Click any color in the palette with the left mouse button to select the drawing color, also known as the foreground color.

2. Click any color with the right mouse button to select the background color.

 tip

When you select a new foreground or background color, the selected colors box (located just to the left of the palette) shows your current selections.

 shortcut

To start a new drawing with a selected background, click the background color with the right mouse button and then choose the New command from the File menu.

note

If you prefer to work with black-and-white patterns rather than colors, choose the Image Attributes command from the Options menu. In the resulting dialog box, select the Black and White option in the Colors box, and click OK. The palette subsequently displays a selection of patterns rather than colors.

To Select a Line Width

Click any of the widths shown in the linesize box. A gray arrow points to the width you have selected.

To Add Text to a Drawing

I. Click the Text tool.

2. Pull down the Text menu one or more times and choose any combination of style options. The options include Bold, Italic, Underline, Outline, and Shadow. When you select an option, a check mark (✔) appears to the left of the option in the menu list.

3. Choose the Fonts command from the Text menu. The resulting Font dialog box contains a font list and a size list, along with other options.

4. Select the name of the font that you want to use for your text entry, and select or enter the point size you want to use. Then click OK.

5. Click the mouse inside the drawing area, at the position where you want to place the text.

6. Type the text from the keyboard. Press Enter at any point where you want to start a new line.

warning

Word-wrap does not take place in text you enter in the drawing area.

To Define and Edit a Cutout

1. Click the Scissors tool to create a freehand cutout, or the Pick tool to create a rectangular cutout.

2. Drag the mouse around the area of your drawing that you want to define as a cutout. A dotted line appears around the cutout area.

3. Perform any of the following actions on the cutout you have defined:

- Position the mouse pointer inside the cutout, hold down either mouse button, and use the mouse to drag the cutout to a new location in the drawing area.

- Hold down the Ctrl key and drag the cutout to make a copy of it at another location.

- Hold down the Shift key and drag the cutout to create multiple copies of the drawing it contains. This is called *sweeping* the cutout.

- Pull down the Pick menu and choose any of the commands that change the contents of the cutout. For example, you can flip the cutout horizontally or vertically, and you can invert the colors of the cutout. You can also make copies of the cutout in larger or smaller sizes, and in angled orientations.

⊚ Press Ctrl+C to copy the cutout to the Clipboard. (You can then paste the drawing into another application.)

4. Click anywhere outside the cutout area to complete your work with the cutout. The dotted line around the cutout disappears.

To Save a Drawing

1. Pull down the File menu and choose the Save As command.

2. In the File Name text box, enter a name for the file you are about to create. (By default, Paintbrush adds BMP as the file's extension name.)

3. Click OK.

 **techno note**

The Save File as Type box in the Save As dialog box offers five dif-ferent formats for the files you create from Paintbrush. In general, a BMP (or *bitmap*) file is the best choice, because this format gives you the ability to use drawings in other Windows applications. (For example, you can place a Paintbrush drawing in a word-processed document that you create in Windows.) But you may sometimes want to create files in a format known as PCX for compatibility with non-Windows software.

shortcut

After you have saved a drawing once, you can save subsquent changes you make in the drawing by choosing the Save command from the File menu.

To Print a Drawing

Choose the Print command from the File menu and click OK on the resulting dialog box.

tip

If you want to print only part of your drawing, click the Partial option in the Print dialog box, and click OK. Paintbrush displays the entire drawing on the screen. Use the mouse to drag a border around the area you want to print, then release the mouse button.

Print Manager

Print Manager is the Windows component that handles printing operations from most applications. When you choose a Print command, the active application sends a file to the Print Manager, which then carries out the job of printing the document.

When the Print Manager is working, its icon appears on the desktop. You never have to open the Print Manager window unless you have a specific reason to do so. The Print Manager does its work in the background while you continue with your work. But sometimes you may want to monitor the Print Manager's current activity.

To Review the Progress of Print Jobs

Double-click the the Print Manager icon on the desktop. The Print Manager window shows you the name of the document it is currently printing, and a queue of documents—if any— that are waiting to be printed.

To Remove a Print Job from the Queue

1. Open the Print Manager window.

2. Select the document you want to remove from the queue.

3. Click the Delete button.

Write

The Write word-processing program contains all the features you're likely to need for writing letters, memos, reports, and other short to medium-length business documents. When you create a document in Write, you can edit the text you have written, format your document in a variety of visually effective ways, and print the document on paper whenever you are ready.

You work on one document at a time in the Write window. To begin a new document, you save your work in the current document, close it, and then start again with an empty Write window. You save Write documents as files with the extension WRI.

Here are some terms you'll need to know as you begin working in Write:

- The *insertion point* is a flashing vertical line (|) that shows you where you are working in your document. When you press a key at the keyboard, the corresponding character appears just to the left of the insertion point, which then moves one position forward for the next character. When you want to insert text in a particular spot in your document, you use the mouse or the arrow keys on the keyboard to reposition the insertion point. (When you point to a position inside the text of a document, the mouse pointer has an I-beam shape.)

- The *end mark* (¤) is a symbol that shows you where the end of your document is.

- The *ruler* is a visual device that helps you change the format of text in your document; it includes icons for spacing between lines, and alignment of paragraphs. (If you want to see the ruler, pull down the Document menu in the Write menu bar and choose Ruler On.)

- *Word wrap* is an event that takes place automatically at the end of each line that you type. When you reach the end of the current line in a given paragraph, Write automatically moves the insertion point to the beginning of the next line. (If the last word you typed is too long to fit on the previous line, Write moves it down to the beginning of the next line.) When you want to start a new paragraph in your document, press the Enter key to move down to the next line, and then press Tab to create an indent if you want one.

⊚ A font is a particular typeface design for the letters and characters of your text. Each font has its own name, such as Times New Roman or Courier. In most Windows applications—including Write—you can select the font in which you want to display and print your text. For a given font selection, you can also change the *style* (*italics*, **boldfacing**, <u>underlining</u>) and the size (also known as *point size*).

To Create a Write Document

1. Open the Accessories group in the Program Manager window and double-click the Write icon. The work area in the Write window is the white space beneath the menu bar; it is initially empty except for the insertion point and the end mark at the upper-left corner. In the title bar of the Write window, the empty document is initially identified as (*Untitled*).

2. Begin typing the text of your document. If you make a mistake, press the Backspace key one or more times to erase the characters you just typed.

3. When you finish typing your document, use the vertical scroll bar to move back to the beginning so you can check your work. (See *Moving Around in a Window* in Part 1 for information about scrolling.) If you need to insert, delete, or change any text within the document, use the mouse to position the insertion point appropriately, and then make any necessary corrections.

4. Pull down the File menu and choose Save As to save your document. (See *To Save a Document* on page 95 for details.)

5. Pull down the File menu and choose Print to print your document. (See *To Print a Document* on page 95 for details.)

6. Pull down the File menu and choose New to close the current document. In response, Write presents you with an empty work area again, ready for your next document.

 reminder

To open an existing Write file from disk, choose Open from the File menu, select the name of the file you want to open, and click OK. To exit the Write program, choose the Exit command from the File menu, or double-click the application window's control-menu box.

To Select Text in a Document

Drag the mouse pointer from the beginning to the end of the text you want to select. Word displays the selection as white text against a black background.

 tip

Before you print a Write document, you can select portions of the text and change the type style of the selection. For example, to emphasize a passage in your text, you might want to select a word or an entire sentence and format it in italics, or format an entire paragraph in boldface.

shortcut

There are several shortcuts you can use to select a word, a sentence, a line, a paragraph, or the entire document:

- To select a word, move the mouse pointer over the word and double-click the mouse button.

- To select a sentence, move the pointer anywhere within the sentence, hold down the Ctrl key, and click the mouse once.

- To select a line, move the mouse pointer into the selection area—the blank column of space just to the left of your document (see Figure 3.3). The pointer takes the shape of a white arrow, pointing diagonally up and to the right. Position the pointer to the right of the line that you want to select and click the mouse once.

- To select a paragraph, move the mouse pointer into the selection area just to the left of the paragraph and double-click the mouse button.

- To select the entire document, move the mouse pointer anywhere in the selection area, hold down the Ctrl key, and click the mouse button once.

To Move or Copy Text

1. Select the text that you want to move or copy.

2. Pull down the Edit menu in the Write menu bar. Choose the Cut command if you want to move the selected text; the selected text disappears from your document. Alternatively, choose the Copy command if you want to make a copy of the selection; the original of the selection remains in the document.

3. Click the mouse or press the arrow keys to move the insertion point to the position where you want to move or copy the selection.

4. Pull down the Edit menu and choose the Paste command.

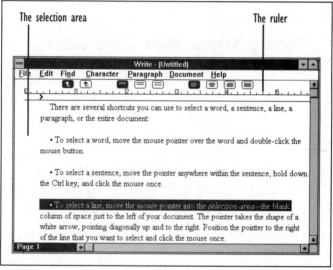

The selection area   The ruler

Write - [Untitled]

File   Edit   Find   Character   Paragraph   Document   Help

> There are several shortcuts you can use to select a word, a sentence, a line, a paragraph, or the entire document:

• To select a word, move the mouse pointer over the word and double-click the mouse button.

• To select a sentence, move the pointer anywhere within the sentence, hold down the Ctrl key, and click the mouse once.

• To select a line, move the mouse pointer into the *selection area*--the blank column of space just to the left of your document. The pointer takes the shape of a white arrow, pointing diagonally up and to the right. Position the pointer to the right of the line that you want to select and click the mouse once.

Page 1

FIGURE 3.3: *Using the selection area of the Word window to select text*

reminder

When you choose the Cut or Copy command in an application, Windows transfers the selection to the Clipboard, where you can view or edit the selection if you wish. (See *Clipboard* on page 71 for more information.)

shortcut

The keyboard shortcut for the Cut command is Ctrl+X. For Copy it is Ctrl+C, and for Paste it is Ctrl+V. These familiar shortcuts are available almost universally in Windows applications.

To Choose Styles, Fonts, and Sizes for Your Text

1. Select the text in which you want to change the style, the font, or the point size. (Select the entire document if you want to change all the text.)

2. Pull down the Character menu in the Write menu bar, and choose one of these commands:

- Choose Bold, Italic, or Underline to change the style of the text.

- Choose Reduce Font or Enlarge Font to decrease or increase the size of the text.

- Choose Fonts to select a new display font for the text. In the resulting Font dialog box, select the name of a font from the Font list, and then click OK.

 tip

You can also use the Font Style list in the Font dialog box to change the style of the selected text, and the Size list to select a new point size.

90

shortcut

Press Ctrl+B to apply boldface to the selection of text. Press Ctrl+I to change the text to italics, or Ctrl+U to underline the text. Press F5 (or choose Regular from the Character menu) to remove boldfacing, italics, and/or underlining from a selection.

To Choose Alignment and Spacing for a Paragraph

1. Move the insertion point to any position inside the paragraph that you want to change. (Select the entire document if you want to change the alignment or spacing for all the text.)

2. Pull down the Paragraph menu and choose one of the following commands to change the alignment:

- ◉ **Left** for alignment at the left border but no alignment at the right (ragged-right text). This is the default.

- ◉ **Centered** for lines that are centered between the left and right margins.

- ◉ **Right** for alignment at the right border but no alignment at the left.

- ◉ **Justified** for alignment at both the left and right borders.

3. Pull down the Paragraph menu and choose Single Space, 1½ Space, or Double Space to change the amount of space within each line of the text.

shortcut

If the ruler is not displayed at the top of the Write window (just below the menu bar), pull down the Document menu and choose the Ruler On command. You'll see a row of icons between the menu bar and the ruler. Click one of the alignment icons (the four icons at the right) to change the alignment of the text, or click one of the spacing icons (the three icons in the middle) to change the spacing between lines.

To Change the Margins of a Document

1. Pull down the Document menu in the Write menu bar, and choose the Page Layout command. The Page Layout dialog box appears on the screen.

2. Enter new measurements in any combination of the Left, Right, Top, and Bottom text boxes.

3. Click OK.

 reminder

The new margins apply to the entire document, not just to a selection of text. By contrast, an indent setting changes the width of a selected paragraph within the current margins.

To Change the Indent Setting of a Paragraph

1. Move the insertion point to any position inside the paragraph that you want to change.

2. Pull down the Paragraph menu and choose Indents.

3. Enter settings for the Left Indent and/or the Right Indent. These settings specify the amount of space by which the width of the paragraph will be indented within the margin settings.

4. Optionally, enter a setting for the First Line indent. This setting specifies the indent for the first line of the paragraph. (A negative number for the First Line setting creates a *hanging indent*, in which the first line of the paragraph starts further to the left than the remaining lines.)

5. Click OK.

 shortcut

If the ruler is not displayed, pull down the Document menu and choose the Ruler On command. The indent markers appear just beneath the ruler; the left- and right-indent markers are triangles, and the first-line indent marker is a dot. Drag these markers to new positions to change the indent settings of the selected paragraph.

To Create a Header or a Footer

1. Pull down the Document menu and choose the Header command to define text that will appear at the top of each printed page, or the Footer command to define text that will appear at the bottom of each page. The text of your document temporarily disappears from the Write window.

2. At the top of the Header or Footer window, type the text that you want to print at the top or bottom of each page.

3. Optionally, click the Insert Page # button in the Page Header or Page Footer dialog box at the position in the text where you want the page number to appear. The notation (*page*) appears in the text of your header or footer.

4. When you complete the text of the header or footer, click the Return to Document button in the Page Header or Page Footer dialog box.

 reminder

The header or footer does not appear on the screen while you are working on the text of your document, but it will be printed on each page of the document. You can edit the header or footer at any time simply by choosing the Header or Footer command from the Document menu. To delete the header or footer, click the Clear button on the Page Header or Page Footer dialog box.

To Save a Document

1. Pull down the File menu and choose the Save As command.

2. In the File Name text box, enter a name for saving the document on disk. (Write automatically supplies the extension WRI.)

3. Click OK.

shortcut

After you have saved a document for the first time, you can simply choose the Save command from the File menu to save subsequent changes you make in the document.

tip

You can instruct Write to make automatic backups of your current document. (A *backup* is a copy of the previously saved version of your document.) To do so, click the Backup check box in the Save As dialog box. Subsequently, Write maintains two versions of your document on disk: the previous version with an extension name of BKP, and the latest version with an extension of WRI.

To Print a Document

1. Pull down the File menu and choose the Print command. The Print dialog box appears on the screen.

2. Optionally, specify the range of pages that you want to print. (The default is All.)

3. Optionally, enter the number of copies that you want to print in the Copies text box. (The default is 1.)

4. Click OK.

 **techno note**

If you need to change the settings for your printer, choose the Print Setup command from the File menu. In the resulting dialog box you can select a printer, and change the page orientation, the paper size, and the source of the paper.

Part 4

File Manager

Introduction

⊚ ⊚

File Manager is a *system application* designed to help you work
with disks, directories, and files on your computer. The icon
for File Manager is located in the Main group of the Program
Manager window.

When you first start File Manager, it displays a *directory window*
with information about files stored on your disk. Figure 4.1
shows an example.

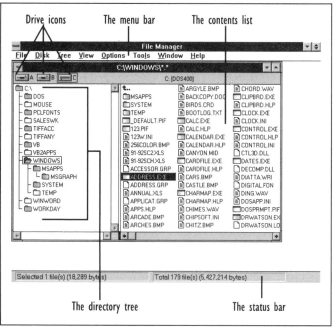

FIGURE 4.1: *The File Manager window*

Directories are a convenient way to organize the space on a
disk. For example, you might create a directory on your hard
disk to store all the files related to a particular task, or all the

files created from a single application. When you create a new directory, you give it a name that indicates the kind of files you plan to store in it. A directory can also contain other directories, for further subdivision of your disk. A directory within a directory is sometimes called a *subdirectory*.

The File Manager directory window is split into two parts:

- The left side of the window shows the *directory tree*—that is, the list of directories and subdirectories—for the current disk. At the top of the directory tree is the *root directory*, represented simply by the drive name and a backslash character (for example, C:\).

- The right side, known as the *contents list*, shows the names of files and subdirectories contained in the current directory. You can use this window to view the contents of any directory on your disk. You can also open additional windows to view different directories side-by-side.

File Manager gives you simple and efficient ways to accomplish a surprising range of tasks. For example, you can:

- Examine detailed information about the files in a directory.

- Copy or move files from one directory to another.

- Open a file in its associated application.

- Print a file.

- Create new directories.

- Format disks.

Part 4 of this book shows you how to accomplish these and other tasks with File Manager.

Starting and Exiting File Manager

Some people use File Manager as a kind of control center for many different activities in Windows. Others open File Manager only occasionally for specific operations related to files and disks. Either way, File Manager is always easy to start.

To Start File Manager

1. Open the Main group in the Program Manager window.

2. Double-click the File Manager icon.

 tip

If you want to open File Manager automatically at the start of each session with Windows, copy its application icon from the Main group to the StartUp group in the Program Manager window. See *Copying a Program Item to a Group* in Part 2 of this book for instructions.

To Exit File Manager

1. Pull down the File menu in the File Manager menu bar.

2. Choose the Exit command.

shortcut

As with other application windows, you can close File Manager quickly by double-clicking the control-menu box at the upper-left corner of the window.

tip

If you want File Manager to display the current arrangement of directory windows next to you start the application, pull down the Options menu and make sure a check mark (✔) is displayed next to the Save Settings on Exit command. (If there is no check mark, choose the command; if there is a check mark, press Esc twice to close the menu.)

Working with Application Files and Document Files

In the contents list—the right side of a directory window—you can view any group of files from a given directory. You might decide you want to view only text files, or only the files created from a particular application. You can also specify the kinds of information you want to see for each file—the name alone, or the name along with other file details. Finally, you can change the order in which the files are displayed—for instance, you can view files in alphabetical order by file name or in numeric order by file size.

Once you have found the group of files you want to work with, you can *select*, or highlight, any number of files in the list. This selection of files then becomes the object of commands that you choose from the File Manager menu bar. For example, you might want to move a group of files from one directory to another, or delete a group of files from the directory.

To View Specific Types of Files in a Directory

1. In the directory tree (at the left side of the directory window) click the directory whose files you want to see. The directory icon—a folder displayed just to the left of the directory name—changes to an open folder. The files from the directory are immediately displayed in the contents list.

2. Pull down the View menu and choose the By File Type command. The resulting dialog box gives you different ways to specify the files you want to see (as shown in Figure 4.2).

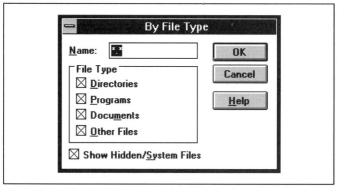

FIGURE 4.2: *The By File Type dialog box*

3. In the Name box, enter a *wildcard* expression for the target files; for example, enter ***.doc** to see all the files with extensions of DOC. (The expression *.* represents all files in the directory.) Alternatively, click any combination of the check boxes in the File Type frame; these options allow you to choose the categories of files that you want to see in the contents list.

4. Click OK. The contents box displays a subset of files that match the specifications you have supplied.

reminder

The wildcard expressions you enter into the By File Type box are the same as those you use in DOS commands.

tip

At the right side of the File Manager's status bar, you can read two items of information about the files currently displayed in the contents list: the number of files, and the total size in bytes of all the files.

To View Specific Information about Files in the Directory Window

1. Pull down the View menu and choose the Partial Details command. The resulting dialog box contains four check boxes, representing the four items of information available for each file—the size in bytes, the last modification date, the last modification time, and the *file attributes*.

2. Place an X in each check box that represents a file detail you want to include in the contents list. (Click a check box once to select it, and again to deselect it.)

3. Click OK to confirm your selection.

 **techno note**

File attributes describe certain technical characteristics of a file: *hidden, read only, archive,* and *system.*

 **shortcut**

If you want to see all the details of each file in the contents list, choose the All File Details command from the View menu. By contrast, choose the Name command from the View menu to see only the file names with no further detail.

To Sort the List of Files in a Directory

Pull down the View menu and choose the Sort command of your choice: Sort by Name, Sort by Type (in other words, by extensions), Sort by Size, or Sort by Date.

 tip

To make sure you can see the relevant information in the contents list, you may need to choose the Partial Details command from the View menu and select the item by which the files are sorted. For example, if the files are arranged in numeric order by file size, make sure the Size option is checked in the Partial Details box.

To Select Files in the Contents List

1. Click the directory whose files you want to select.
(Optionally, choose the By File Type command from
the View menu to choose the types of files that you
want to display in the contents list.)

2. Use one of the following techniques to select a group
of files in the contents list:

⊙ To select one file, click the file's name with the
mouse.

⊙ To select a group of files out of sequence, hold
down the Ctrl key while you select each file in the
group.

⊙ To select a group of two or more files in sequence,
click the first file and then hold down the Shift key
and click the last file in the sequence.

⊙ To select two or more groups of files in sequence
(as illustrated in Figure 4.3), select the first group as
described above; then for each subsequent group,
hold down the Ctrl key while you click the first file
in the group and hold down the Shift and Ctrl keys
together while you click the last file in the group.

shortcut

To select files by type, choose the Select Files command
from the File menu. Enter a wildcard expression (for example,
*.txt) in the File(s) box. Click the Select button and then
the Close button.

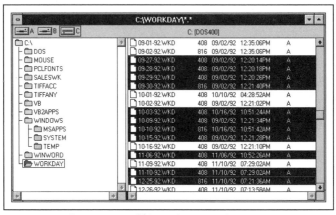

FIGURE 4.3: *Selecting groups of files in the contents list*

tip

To deselect a single file, hold down the Ctrl key and click the highlighted file. To deselect all groups of highlighted files at once, hold down the Ctrl key and press the backslash (\) key or just let go of Ctrl and click a file.

reminder

Once you have selected one or more files in the contents list, you can choose commands from the File Manager menu bar to perform specific operations on the selected files.

To Copy Files from One Directory to Another

1. In the directory tree, click the name of the directory from which you want to copy the files. This is the *source* directory.

2. In the contents list of the source directory, select the file or files that you want to copy.

3. Hold down the Ctrl key and drag the selection to the name of the *destination* directory in the directory tree— that is, the directory to which you are copying the file or files. While you are dragging, the mouse pointer takes the shape of a document icon with a plus sign inside it.

4. Release the mouse button and then the Ctrl key when the pointer is positioned over the destination directory. A message box titled Confirm Mouse Operation appears on the screen. Click Yes to confirm the copy operation. File Manager copies the selected files to the target directory.

5. Click the target directory and examine the contents list to make sure that the files were copied as expected.

 tip

If you want to be able to see both the source and destination directories while you are completing a copy operation, open up a second directory window for the destination by choosing New Window from the Window menu. Then choose Tile from the Window menu to arrange the two open windows more conveniently. See *Working with Directories* on page 111 for more information.

tip

You can copy a selection of files to a disk in another drive by dragging the selection to the disk icon at the top of the directory window or by dragging the selection into another window you've opened for the destination drive (see Figure 4.1 on page 98). You do not need to hold down the Ctrl key in this case.

To Move Files from One Directory to Another

1. In the directory tree, click the name of the directory from which you want to move the files. This is the *source* directory.

2. In the contents list of the source directory, select the file or files that you want to move.

3. Drag the selection to the name of the *destination* directory in the directory tree—that is, the directory to which you want to move the file or files. While you are dragging, the mouse pointer takes the shape of a document icon.

4. Release the mouse button when the pointer is positioned over the destination directory. A message box titled Confirm Mouse Operation appears on the screen. Click Yes to confirm the move operation. File Manager moves the selected files to the destination directory. The file names no longer appear in the contents list for the original source directory.

5. Click the target directory and examine the contents list to make sure that the files were moved as expected.

tip

You can *move* files from one drive to another by holding down the Shift key and dragging the selected files to the destination drive icon or window. The files are erased from the source drive as a result of this operation. To *copy* files from one drive to another, drag the files without holding down Shift.

To Print a Document File from File Manager

1. Open the Main group in the Program Manager window and double-click the Print Manager icon. When the Print Manager window opens, click its minimize button to display it as an icon on the desktop.

2. Activate and open the File Manager window and select the name of the document file that you want to print.

3. Drag the file from the contents list to the Print Manager icon on the desktop. To print the file, Windows temporarily opens the application in which the file was originally created (or the application with which the file was subseqently associated).

shortcut

Select a file in the contents list, and choose the Print command from the File Manager's File menu. Then click OK on the Print dialog box.

 **techno note**

If File Manager cannot determine an appropriate application from which to print the file, a message box titled Cannot Print File appears on the screen. Click OK in the message box, and then choose the Associate command from the File menu to select an application for printing the file. In the Files with Extension box, enter the extension name of the files that you want to associate with a particular application. In the Associate With list, click an application from which files of this type can be printed. Then click OK.

To Start an Application from File Manager

Double-click an application (for example, an EXE or COM file) in the contents list.

To Start an Application and Open a Document

Double-click the document file in the contents list.

To Delete a File from a Disk

1. In the directory tree, click the directory from which you want to delete a file.

2. In the contents list for the directory, select the file that you want to delete.

3. Choose the Delete command from the File menu, or press Del from the keyboard.

4. In the Delete dialog box, click OK.

5. In the Confirm File Delete dialog box, click Yes.

tip

If you want to delete more than one file in a single operation, select all the files you want to delete and press Del.

To Rename a File

1. In the contents list, select the file that you want to rename.

2. Choose Rename from the File menu.

3. In the Rename dialog box, enter the new name for the file into the To box.

4. Click OK.

warning

Rename only your own document files. Do not rename files that are required for the operations of a particular application.

Working with Directories

File Manager simplifies and clarifies a number of directory-related tasks that are typically performed in DOS. For example, you can easily create a new directory at any level of a directory tree. In addition, the File Manager allows you to look at the contents of two or more directories side-by-side—which cannot be done from the DOS prompt.

To View Multiple Directory Windows at Once

1. Pull down the Window menu in the File Manager menu bar and choose the New Window command. A new directory window appears inside the File Manager window.

2. In the directory tree of the new window, click the directory that you want to view in this window.

3. Repeat steps 1 and 2 for as many new directory windows as you want to open.

 tip

Pull down the Window menu and choose Tile or Cascade to rearrange the open directory windows. Tile arranges the windows side by side and resizes the windows appropriately. Cascade arranges the windows in an overlapping stack.

To Create a New Directory

1. In the directory tree, select the directory level where you want to create the new directory. To create a directory in the root directory, select the backslash (\) at the top of the tree. To create a subdirectory within a directory, select the name of the target directory in the tree.

2. Pull down the File menu and choose Create Directory.

3. In the Create Directory dialog box, enter a name for the new directory you are creating. (Also, make sure that the Current Directory label correctly identifies the level where you want to create the new directory.)

4. Click OK.

tip

To view the names of the subdirectories of a given directory, double-click the directory's name in the tree. This is called *expanding* the directory tree. Conversely, you can *collapse* the directory by double-clicking its name in the tree again.

Working with Drives and Disks

⊚ ⊚

File Manager gives you the tools you need to perform everyday disk operations without exiting Windows.

To View Files or Directories on a Selected Drive

Click the drive icon at the top of the directory window (see Figure 4.1 on page 98).

To Format a Floppy Disk in a Selected Drive

1. Insert a floppy disk in the appropriate disk drive.

2. Pull down the Disk menu and choose Format Disk. The Format Disk dialog box appears on the screen.

3. In the Disk In box, choose the name of the drive that contains the disk to be formatted.

4. In the Capacity box, choose the memory capacity of the disk you have inserted in the drive.

5. Optionally, enter a label (of up to 11 characters) for the disk in the Label box.

6. If you want to copy *system files* to the disk, click the Make System Disk option.

7. Click OK. File Manager displays a message box in which you can monitor the progress of the formatting operation.

8. When the operation is finished, the Format Complete message box appears on the screen. Click Yes or No in response to the question *Do you want to format another disk?*

 **techno note**

A system disk (also known as a *start-up disk*) contains DOS files required for initially starting your computer. These include two hidden files, plus the file named COMMAND.COM.

To Copy System Files to a Disk That Is Already Formatted

1. Insert the disk in the appropriate drive.

2. Pull down the Disk menu and choose Make System Disk.

3. In the *Copy System Files to Disk* in box, select the drive where you have inserted the disk.

4. Click OK.

 warning

If you have already stored files on a non-system disk, File Manager will not be able to copy the system files to the disk. This is because the two hidden system files must be copied to specific locations on the disk.

114

Part 5

Control Panel

Introduction

⊚ ⊚

In Windows' Control Panel, you can change the settings that
control the way Windows looks and behaves on your computer. You open Control Panel by double-clicking the Control
Panel icon in the Main group of the Program Manager window. As shown in Figure 5.1, the Control Panel window displays icons representing different categories of settings. When
you double-click one of these icons, a dialog box presents the
options available in the category you have chosen.

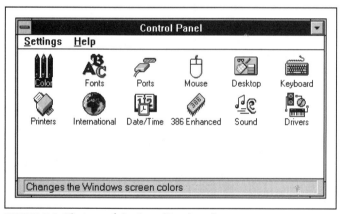

FIGURE 5.1: *The icons of the Control Panel window*

Part 5 shows you the procedures for changing a selection of
important settings.

 **techno note**

The current settings for Windows on your computer are stored on
disk in a text file named WIN.INI. When you change any Control

116

Panel settings, Windows revises the appropriate lines of this file. The new settings then remain in effect each time you start Windows unless you change them again during a subsequent session.

Color Settings

For improved readability—or just for variety—you can change the colors of the Windows screen. One way to do this is to choose one of the twenty or so color schemes that Windows defines. Another way is to create your own color scheme by choosing colors for individual parts of the screen.

To Select a Predesigned Color Scheme

1. Open the Main group in the Program Manager window and double-click the Control Panel icon.

2. Double-click the Color icon in the Control Panel. The resulting dialog box contains a list of predefined color schemes, along a sample screen box that shows you how your screen will appear when you choose a particular color scheme.

3. Click the down-arrow button at the right side of the Color Schemes box to view the list. The color schemes have names such as Wingtips, Cinnamon, and Emerald City.

4. Select a color scheme and examine its color combinations in the sample screen.

5. Repeat step 4 any number of times with different selections until you find a color combination you like.

6. Click the OK button at the bottom of the Color dialog box. The dialog box closes, and your Windows screen now displays the color combinations you have selected.

tip

You can always return to the original colors by choosing Windows Default in the Color Schemes list.

To Create a Customized Color Scheme

1. Open the Control Panel window and double-click the Color icon.

2. Click the Color Palette button near the bottom of the Color dialog box. The box expands to show a grid of the standard colors available for the Windows screen (see Figure 5.2).

3. Click any element of the sample screen box at the left side of the Color dialog box. For example, click the title bar of the active window, the menu bar, the command button, or the scroll bar. Your selection is identified in the Screen Element box in the upper-right corner of the Color dialog box.

4. Click a color in the palette. This color is immediately applied to the element you selected in the sample screen.

5. Repeat steps 3 and 4 for each screen element whose color you want to change.

6. Click the OK button. The Windows screen displays the new colors you have selected.

 tip

If you find it difficult to select screen elements in the sample screen box, you can instead choose an element by name from the Screen Element list. Click the down-arrow button at the right side of the list, and select the name of the element whose

118

color you want to change.

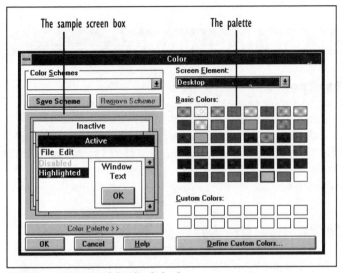

FIGURE 5.2: *The expanded Color dialog box*

 tip

If you find it difficult to select screen elements in the sample
screen box, you can instead choose an element by name from
the Screen Element list. Click the down-arrow button at the
right side of the list, and select the name of the element whose
color you want to change.

 note

When you design a custom color screen that you like, you can
save it as an option in the Color Schemes list. Click the Save

Scheme button on the Color dialog box, and then supply a
name for your scheme in the box that appears on the screen.

Date and Time Settings

Your computer has an internal clock and calendar that you can
reset whenever necessary. These settings are important in a
variety of ways. For example, the system's current time and
date are recorded along with the file name whenever you save
a file to disk. In addition, applications such as Calendar and Clock
(in the Accessories group) rely on the system clock to provide
you with specific information about the current date and time.

To Change the System Date and Time

1. Open the Main group in the Program Manager window, and double-click the Control Panel icon.

2. In the Control Panel window, double-click the
Date/Time icon. A small dialog box showing the
current date and time appears on the screen.

3. Choose the date or time element that you want to
change—the month, day, or year in the Date box,
or the hour, minutes, or seconds in the Time box.
(Double-click any one of these elements to highlight it.)

4. Click the appropriate up-arrow button to increase the
element you have selected, or the down-arrow button
to decrease it.

5. Repeat steps 3 and 4 for any other date or time elements that you want to change.

6. Click OK to confirm the new settings. Windows resets
the system clock and calendar accordingly.

120

Fonts

Fonts are the typefaces available for you to use in Windows documents. There are several types of fonts in Windows, but the most useful are known as TrueType fonts. The advantage of these is that they appear the same on the screen as they do when you print them on paper.

The Control Panel's Fonts dialog box lets you examine the fonts already installed for use in Windows and install additional fonts that you may purchase on disk. The dialog box contains a list of the names of installed fonts, and a sample box for displaying text in a selected font. It also contains several command buttons that you can click to perform operations with fonts.

To View a Sample of an Installed Font

1. Open the Main group in the Program Manager window, and double-click the Control Panel icon.

2. In the Control Panel window, double-click the Fonts icon to open the Fonts dialog box.

3. Select the name of an installed font that you want to examine. A sample of the font appears in the box located just below the Installed Fonts list.

4. Click Cancel to close the Fonts dialog box.

 note

In the Installed Fonts list, each font is identified both by name and by type. As you look down the list, notice the fonts identified as TrueType. These are the best ones to use in most

Windows applications.

To Install New Fonts for Use in Windows

1. If you are installing new fonts from a floppy disk, insert the disk in the appropriate drive.

2. Double-click the Control Panel icon in the Main group, and then double-click the Fonts icon.

3. In the Fonts dialog box, click the Add button. The Add Fonts dialog box appears on the screen.

4. Click the down-arrow button at the right side of the Drives box and select the drive from which you are installing the fonts. If necessary, use the Directories box to select the directory where the fonts are located. The font names appear in the List of Fonts box.

5. If you want to install all the fonts listed, click the Select All button. Otherwise, select the names of fonts that you want to install.

6. Make sure the Copy Fonts to Windows Directory box is checked. (Click it if it is not.)

7. Click OK on the Add Fonts dialog box. When the fonts are copied, the Fonts dialog box reappears, and the names of new fonts appear in the Installed Fonts list.

8. Click the Close button to close the Fonts dialog box.

Desktop Settings

The Desktop dialog box gives you some useful and amusing ways to change the way your desktop looks and behaves.

When you first see this dialog box, you may be confused by the large assortment of options it contains (see Figure 5.3). But the settings in this dialog box are worth examining carefully, because each results in a significant change in your Windows configuration.

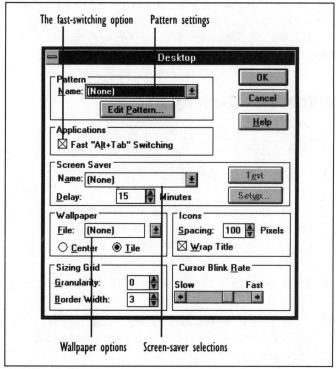

The fast-switching option   Pattern settings

Wallpaper options   Screen-saver selections

FIGURE 5.3: *The Desktop settings*

For example, if you're tired of the plain gray background that always appears behind your application windows, you can design and apply a pattern to the desktop surface. Or you can even select a "wallpaper" design for the desktop background.

More important than these visual options, the Desktop dialog box offers you a selection of *screen savers*. A screen saver is a graphic pattern that takes over your screen when you've been away from your computer for a time—for example, when you go off on a lunch break, or when you are out of your office at a meeting. The constantly changing pattern of the screen saver prevents damage to the screen itself. When you come back to your computer and are ready to return to Windows, you simply move the mouse or press a key on the keyboard. The screen saver disappears and you once again see your work on the desktop.

To Choose a Desktop Pattern

1. Open the Main group in the Program Manager window, and double-click the Control Panel icon.

2. Double-click the Desktop icon. The Desktop dialog box appears.

3. In the Pattern frame, click the down-arrow button at the right side of the Name box. A list of patterns appears on the screen. The patterns have whimsical names such as Paisley, Scottie, Tulip, and Waffle.

4. Select a pattern from the list, and then click OK on the Desktop dialog box.

5. Take a look at the resulting pattern on the Windows desktop. If you don't like it, go back to step 2 and select a new pattern.

 tip

If you decide you want to go back to the plain gray desktop, choose (None) in the Pattern list.

To Create Your Own Desktop Pattern

1. Double-click the Desktop icon in the Control Panel window.

2. In the Patterns list, choose the name of a pattern to use as the starting point for your custom pattern. Choose (None) if you want to start with a blank pattern screen.

3. Click the Edit Pattern button. The Desktop—Edit Pattern dialog box appears; it contains a sample of the way the pattern is currently designed to appear on the desktop, and an enlarged pattern box in which you can edit the pattern.

4. Inside the enlarged pattern box, click the locations where you want to reverse the color. With each click, the sample box immediately shows how the revised pattern will look on the desktop.

5. When you have completed your work on the pattern, enter a name for the new pattern in the Name text box.

6. Click the Add button to add this new pattern to the Pattern list, then click OK to close the Edit Pattern dialog box.

7. Click OK in the Desktop dialog box to apply this new pattern to the Windows desktop.

 tip

If you prefer to revise the current pattern instead of creating a pattern under a new name, click the Change button on the Edit Pattern dialog box.

To Choose a Screen Saver

1. Double-click the Desktop icon in the Control Panel window.

2. In the Screen Saver frame, click the down-arrow button next to the Name box. A list of the available screen savers appears on the screen.

3. Select one of the screen savers, and then click the Test button to see what it looks like on the screen. To return to Windows, move the mouse or press a key on the keyboard.

4. Repeat step 3 if you want to test other screen savers before making your final selection.

5. If you want, enter a new number in the Delay box. This is the number of minutes Windows will wait before starting the screen saver on your unattended computer.

6. Click OK in the Desktop dialog box to confirm your selection.

To Change the Characteristics of a Screen Saver

Follow steps 1 through 5 in the previous task, and then click the Setup button. The resulting dialog box presents a variety of options related to the screen saver that you have chosen. Make any changes in the screen saver settings, and then click OK.

 **techno note**

You can define a password to go with most screen savers. Whenever the screen saver takes over, you must supply the password correctly in order to return to Windows.

If you want to create a password for your selected screen

saver, check the Password Protected option in the Setup dialog box and then click the Set Password button. Type the password in the resulting dialog box.

warning

A password effectively prevents other people from using your computer while you are away, but it will also prevent you from using your own computer if you forget the correct word.

To Choose a Wallpaper

1. Double-click the Desktop icon in the Control Panel window.

2. In the Wallpaper frame, click the down-arrow button to view the list of wallpaper files.

3. Select a file from the list, or click (None) if you want to remove an existing wallpaper selection.

4. Choose the Center option if you want the wallpaper pattern to appear only once in the center of the desktop, or click Tile if you want the entire desktop to be covered with the wallpaper pattern.

5. Click OK. The new wallpaper pattern appears on the desktop.

To Activate or Deactivate the Fast-Switching Feature

The fast-switching feature is a quick way to switch from one running application to another in Windows. When this feature is activated, you can press Alt+Tab repeatedly to step through the applications on the desktop, and then release the Alt key to activate the application of your choice. (See *Switching to Another Application* in Part 1 of this book for more information.)

If this feature does not work on your computer, it has been turned off in the Desktop settings of the Control Panel.

Follow these steps to turn fast-switching on or off:

1. Double-click the Desktop icon in the Control Panel window.

2. In the Applications frame, click the check box labeled Fast "Alt+Tab" Switching. (If this box is checked, fast-switching is active; if the box is unchecked, the feature does not work.)

3. Click OK.

Mouse Settings

The Mouse settings in the control panel let you change the way the mouse works in Windows. The Mouse dialog box contains two scroll bars representing speed settings:

- The Mouse Tracking Speed setting determines how fast the mouse pointer travels across the screen when you move the mouse.

- The Double Click Speed setting determines how fast you have to click the mouse in order to record a double-click.

Two check boxes in the Mouse dialog box represent other options. One of these options changes the appearance of the mouse pointer itself. But possibly the most significant setting in this category is the one that allows you to swap the use of the left and right buttons on the mouse. If you are a left-handed mouse user, this option can significantly improve the effectiveness of the mouse as an input device.

warning

All of the mouse settings go into effect as soon as you change them in the Mouse dialog box. This means that you can test the effect of each new setting as soon as you change it. It also means that the new setting affects the way you use the Mouse dialog box itself. Keep this in mind especially if you make a change in the left-right orientation of the mouse buttons.

To Change the Speed Settings

1. Open the Main group in the Program Manager window, and double-click the Control Panel icon.

2. In the Control Panel window, double-click the Mouse icon. The Mouse dialog box appears on the screen.

3. In the Mouse Tracking Speed scroll bar, drag the scroll box toward Fast to increase the speed at which the mouse pointer travels relative to the mouse movement. Drag the scroll box toward Slow to decrease the speed.

4. In the Double Click Speed scroll bar, drag the scroll box toward Fast to increase the speed required for a double-click or toward Slow to decrease the speed.

5. To test the current clicking speed, double-click the mouse pointer over the Test button. The button changes color if your double-clicking is fast enough to meet the requirements of the current setting.

6. Click OK to confirm the new speed settings.

To Change the Left-Right Orientation of the Mouse Buttons

1. Double-click the Mouse icon in the Control Panel window.

2. In the Mouse dialog box, click the check box labeled Swap Left/Right Buttons to exchange the roles of the left and right mouse buttons. When you change this option, the mouse box just above the option shows you the current orientation of the buttons. (When the box is unchecked, the left mouse button is the standard button to use for selecting objects on the screen; when it is checked, the right button becomes the standard.)

To Activate Mouse Trails

1. Double-click the Mouse icon in the Control Panel window.

2. Click the Mouse Trails check box. A check in this box means that mouse trails will appear.

3. Move the mouse around the screen to test the feature. If you like the effect, keep the option checked; if not, remove the check.

 tip

When the Mouse Trails option is checked, the mouse pointer leaves a trail of shadow pointers as it travels across the screen. This can be useful on screens where the mouse pointer is not as clearly visible as you would like it to be (laptops, for example).

INDEX

Boldface page numbers indicate definitions and principal discussions of primary topics and subtopics. *Italic* page numbers indicate illustrations.

Symbols

\ (backslash character), 99
✓ (check mark), 8, 45, 80, 101
... (ellipses), **12**
¤ (end mark), **85**
| (vertical line), **85**

A

About Program Manager
       command, 58
Access, 34
Accessories group, **33–34**,
      65, 86
   Calendar and, 61
   Control Panel and, 120
   Notepad and, 74
   Paintbrush and, 76
Add button, 122, 125
Add command, 67
Add dialog box, 67
Add Fonts dialog box, 122
Airbrush, 76, 78
All File Details command, 104
applications, **2**
   active, **2**

closing, **19–22**
icons representing, 4
starting, **15**
switching to other, **15–19**
system, **33**
Applications frame, 128
Applications group, **33–34**
archive attribute, 104
Arrange icons command, 45
Auto Arrange command, 45
AUTOEXEC.BAT, **7**, 52, 74

B

backslash character (\), 99
Backup check box, 95
backup files, **95**
bitmap files, 82
Black and White option, 80
Bold option, 80
boldface, 86, **91–92**
Box (Paintbrush tool), 76
Browse button, 36, 47
Browse dialog box, 36, 37, 47
Brush, 76, 78
By File Type command, 102, 105
By File Type dialog box, 102, 103

Q

R

ruler, 85, 89
    displaying, 92, 93
Ruler On command, 92, 93
Run command, **2**, **14–15**, **34–38**.
    See also running
running. *See also* Run command
    applications automatically,
        37–38
    applications represented by
        icons, **10–11**, **35**
    multiple applications, 29
    opening documents
        automatically when,
        51–52
Run dialog box, 36, 37
Run Minimized box, 35, **36**

S

Save As command, 61, 65, 74,
    77, 82, 86, 95
Save As dialog box, 61, 74
Save command, 19, 83, 95
Save File as Type box, 82
Save Scheme button, 119–120
Save Settings command, 101
saving. *See also* backup files
    before closing applications, **19**
    changes before exiting, 7
    Paintbrush drawings, **82**
    Program Manager before
        exiting, **8**
    Write documents, **95**
Scissors Tool, 76, 78
    defining and editing cutouts
        with, **81–82**
Screen Element box, 118
Screen Element list, 119–120

Screen Saver frame, 126
Screen savers, **123–124**
    changing characteristics of,
        126–127
    choosing, **126**
    creating passwords for,
        126–127
scroll bars, **28**. *See also* scrolling
scrolling
    through card files, **69**
    to new dates, **62**
    vertically and horizontally,
        28–29
    in Write documents, 86
Search button, 57
Search dialog box, 57
Search for Help command, 57
searching
    for card files, **68**
    for files on hard disks, **36–37**
    for information about
        features, **57**
    for programs in directories, **47**
    for text in the Cardfile
        information area, **69**
Search menu, 68, 69
Select All button, 122
Select button, 105
Select Files command, 105
selection area, 89
Set Password button, 127
Setup dialog box, 127
Shadow option, 80
Shortcut Key text box, 46, 52
Show Date dialog box, 62
Show menu, 62
Show Topics button, 57
Size command, **27**
Size option, 104